Keeping Something Alive

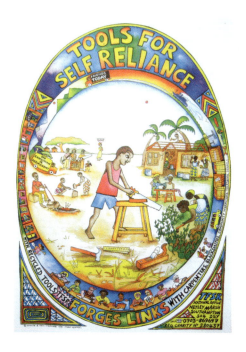

Keeping Something Alive

THE STORY OF
TOOLS FOR SELF RELIANCE

ITS ORIGINS AND EARLY YEARS 1978 – 1995

Owen – our friendship spans so many years! Good to meet up again.
Glyn 25.10.08.

Glyn Roberts
AND **Mark Smith**

Published by **Brill Books**, 2008.

ISBN: 978-1-906274-07-8

© Glyn Roberts and Mark Smith

Further copies available from **Tools for Self Reliance**, Netley Marsh, Southampton SO40 7GY
Telephone: 02380 869697, info@tfsr.org

All proceeds from sales to Tools for Self Reliance

Design & Print: **Studio 6**, The Square, Wickham, Hampshire, PO17 5JN
Telephone: 01329 832933 • www.studio-6.co.uk

DVD design & processing: Maurice Gilliam • www.mauricegilliam.co.uk

Printed on paper from sustainable sources

If you'd like to get in touch with Glyn or Mark about any issues raised in the book, please email **keepingsomethingalive@yahoo.co.uk** or contact us by letter, c/o Tools for Self Reliance.

Why *Keeping Something Alive*?

Our title comes from a comment made years ago by Johnny Buck of the **Bradford Woodworkers' Cooperative**. Working long hours to make and market furniture, they still found time to collect and refurbish tools for carpenters in Nicaragua.

Johnny told us, 'Sometimes, even here, we end up feeling like part of some industrial production process – it grinds you down. But I think that supporting a small group in a village project abroad – it keeps something alive in Me about the sort of world I want to live in.'

For us, this captures the spirit of practical solidarity that has inspired Tools for Self Reliance. Also, giving old tools a new lease of life helps to sustain artisan communities overseas. And by refurbishing tools and passing on their skills, hundreds of older helpers in Britain find a new purpose to life in their retirement years.

'All modern technology depends ultimately on basic hand tools... Most men and women on this planet still grow their food and earn their living using such tools... They may seem old fashioned, but in fact they are highly productive and amazingly versatile. They cause very little damage, pollution or waste. They do not depend on fossil fuels. They are truly cost-effective, they sustain employment and are 'power-sharing' politically. Has any other technology such a catalogue of good qualities?'

TFSR STATEMENT TO THE UNITED NATIONS
CONFERENCE ON ENVIRONMENT & DEVELOPMENT,
GENEVA, 1990

FRONT COVER PHOTOGRAPH Mr JS Malecela, High Commissioner of Tanzania, helps Harry, Colin and Xavier load a container with tools (1990). Photo courtesy of *Southern Evening Echo*.
HALF-TITLE PAGE ILLUSTRATION Courtesy Ken and Annie Meharg.
TITLE PAGE PHOTOGRAPH *Trompe l'œil* entrance to Garvald tools workshop, Edinburgh. Photo courtesy of Paul Turner.

CONTENTS

Foreword	8
Introduction	10
The Origins of TFSR	12
The Early Days, 1979 – 1983	18
The Crisis Years, 1984 – April 1986	44
Growth and Consolidation, May 1986 – 1990	60
Towards the new Millennium, 1991 – 1995	84
The Early Years in Hindsight	110
Reflections on the past… and the future?	122
Appendix: Tools totals, 1979 – 1995	127

LEFT Kisokwe Blacksmith's Group, Tanzania (1992).

Foreword

WE HAVE WRITTEN THIS BOOK in the third person, rather than the first, using 'Mark' and 'Glyn' when referring to ourselves. This sometimes felt slightly forced, but a choice had to be made and on balance we think that it reads better this way.

Hundreds of groups and organisations, and thousands of individuals supported Tools for Self Reliance (TFSR) in different ways between 1978 and 1995. Obviously, we can mention only a limited number by name, but we pay tribute here to the very many others who played a part. Their hard work, generosity, good advice, commitment, sense of fun and occasional sharp criticism, all helped TFSR go from strength to strength.

We know that some disapprove of the terms, but we decided to use North, when referring to the 'Western' industrialised nations, and South or the Third World to cover the economically deprived countries of Africa, Asia and Latin America.

The story unfolds year by year, January to December, but statistics for tools output and finances follow TFSR's financial year, September to August. It was simply too tedious to point this out each time in the text.

We are grateful to The Joseph Rowntree Charitable Trust, which has supported TFSR from its very early days, for funding the publication of this book.

Finally, our thanks to the team at Studio 6, especially Alistair Plumb and Lindsey Maguire, for their enthusiasm and hard work in designing and printing this book.

> 'The African peasant entered colonialism with a hoe
> and came out of it with a hoe.
> It is clear now, however,
> that the hoe he carried into colonialism
> was locally produced,
> while the one coming out was imported.'
>
> WALTER RODNEY
> *HOW EUROPE UNDERDEVELOPED AFRICA*

FOREWORD

The only two saws owned by a village cooperative of 28 men.
Nzunguni, Tanzania, (1983)

Introduction

IT IS NOW THIRTY YEARS since the launch of Tools for Self Reliance. Over this time TFSR has touched the lives of many, not only through equipping communities overseas with millions of tools*, but by doing so in a spirit of what might be called 'friendly solidarity'.

Our aim was never to create yet another technical assistance scheme. We certainly believed that sending out refurbished tools would be useful, as would training courses in skills development or marketing for small businesses in Africa. But shouldn't we try to do more? Using the 'tools' idea, couldn't we forge links of understanding between people and organisations in the North and South, make personal contact, share experiences and together highlight the forces that connect wealth, power and poverty? Could we bring evidence from the field to convince people, especially policy-makers in overseas aid, that 'development on a human scale' is what matters? And in the wider context, shouldn't we be taking a stand on such issues as waste, Third World debt, the arms trade, pollution... which more than cancel out the benefits that overseas aid may bring?

Having worked as, and with volunteers, we wanted TFSR to be volunteer-based because we knew of their great energy, enthusiasm and integrity. However, we also knew that to count on their spirit, our organisation itself must be open, friendly and frugal – yet also competent.

Since 1978, thousands have helped TFSR and its partner organisations overseas. Sadly, several of the veterans and some of our overseas partners are no longer alive, but new generations of activists carry on the work with energy and commitment. Today, some of these may wonder from time to time, as they de-rust hammers on a rainy day in Britain or unpack crates under an African sun, 'How did TFSR actually begin?'

This book is for you, and for the people, funders, organisations and partners who have worked with TFSR over the years. It recalls what inspired Tools for Self Reliance, how and why it came into being, and the effort, ferment and

---

* The overall total is unknown, and may not even be particularly important, but TFSR, plus the tools groups in Europe and Asia inspired by TFSR, plus the many blacksmiths in Africa assisted by TFSR – all together will have generated several millions by 2008.

crises of those early years. The final section assesses how far we stuck to our principles and realised or failed to match up to the early hopes.

Our story may also have a wider significance. Britain is unique in the strength and extent of the voluntary sector to which TFSR belongs. The 1970s saw the launch of numerous non-governmental organisations (NGOs). Some of them are still around today, but many are long gone. How do small voluntary organisations start, develop, face crises and sink or swim? This book is a case study of one such NGO. It does not try to assess the impact of all the tools in the 28 countries to which they went – an impossible task, three decades on – though we do refer to evaluation made by TFSR and its partners during the years in question.

Besides our own recollections, we have drawn on documents, photographs and videos from the TFSR archives and have asked others to contribute their memories. But, in the last resort, this is a personal account of an exciting period in our lives, inevitably selective, and responsibility for omissions and any errors must lie with us.

Glyn Roberts and **Mark Smith** October, 2008

'Man is a Tool-making animal...
weak in himself, nevertheless he can
use Tools, can devise Tools...
With these he kneads glowing iron as if it was soft paste.
Nowhere do you find him without Tools;
without Tools he is nothing,
with Tools he is all.'

THOMAS CARLYLE

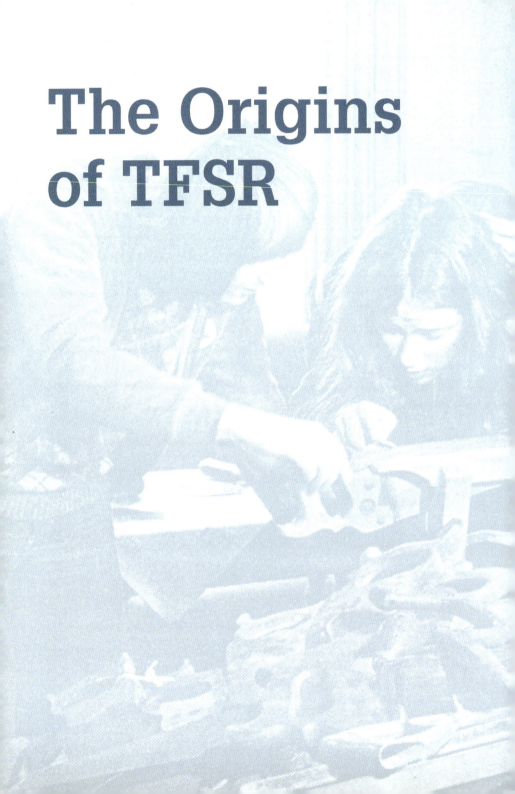

The Origins of TFSR

TOOLS FOR SELF RELIANCE sprang, not from an interest in technology, but from the spirit and values of volunteering. From the 1960s onwards, many, mainly young, people from Northern countries volunteered for service in the Third World. The American Peace Corps and British programmes such as VSO had their critics, but they did enable thousands of volunteers to live and work alongside local teachers, nurses, mechanics and similar skilled workers in Africa, Asia and Latin America. They were motivated not by high salaries, but by the wish to be useful, and for many it was a life-changing experience.

A good number returned home determined to 'do something more for a fairer world', and had grounds for believing it possible. In particular, many volunteers like Mark Smith working in Tanzania had been attracted to its development philosophy (*ujamaa*) based on values of equality, cooperation, socialism and self-reliance. The country's *Arusha Declaration* (1967) called for principled behaviour by all its citizens, including the leadership. Tanzania's brave attempts to implement fair policies (even if certain programmes did later go off the rails) and various books and speeches by Mwalimu Julius Nyerere* showed that a government actually could make the poor a priority.

Glyn Roberts was particularly moved by Tanzania's approach because he had travelled in Africa and Asia and seen terrible poverty next to obscene wealth in country after country, often alongside costly and ineffective Aid projects. In Ethiopia there had been giant Caterpillar diggers rusting away, part of a road-building project – no diesel, no spare parts. Middle class Ethiopians did well out of such schemes, but thousands of ordinary citizens, desperate for work, went unemployed and hungry. He'd watched foreign companies in West Africa suck out raw materials in the name of modernisation, their expatriate staff pampered by servants, their salaries, air-conditioned Range Rovers and perks all adding to Third World debt. Time

---

* Julius K Nyerere (1922–1999) – philosopher, statesman and teacher – led Tanganyika to independence in 1961 and became first president of Tanzania after the union with Zanzibar in 1964. After four times being re-elected, he retired in 1985, but continued as Chairman of *Chama Cha Mapinduzi* (then Tanzania's only political party) until 1990. Although Head of State for so many years, he was widely referred to by the title he preferred, *Mwalimu*, meaning 'teacher'.

and again, their power and technology dispossessed ordinary working people of rights, land and resources.

Back in the UK, Glyn published several short books, mainly for volunteers going abroad, including *Volunteers and Neo-colonialism* (1968) and *Questioning Development* (1974). These argued that 1. genuine development means empowering those at the bottom of the social pyramid; 2. ordinary people in the North and South share a common interest in this empowerment; and 3. organisations working against poverty and powerlessness (especially *volunteer* organisations) should themselves be frugal and democratic*.

The books, for a long time recommended reading for young people going to the South, caused some debate in volunteer circles, and Glyn was challenged at one conference by Frank Judd MP (later Minister for Overseas Development) to go beyond writing books and try putting these principles into practice. 'Start an organisation,' he said, 'and you will find that keeping to ideals is not so easy. You too will have to make compromises...' Stung by Frank's words, he left the conference determined to come up with a strong idea, some form of useful action that would embody these principles, but for years nothing caught his imagination.

Then, one evening at a teachers' training college in central Uganda, he heard a foreign aid expert complain that students were helping themselves to hand tools from his precious visual aid display. 'They're born thieves,' he muttered over a beer, 'No sooner do I turn my back, but they nick a chisel. Next it's a saw; then a brace & bit... and these are demonstration tools – not to be *used*!'

A visit to village craftsmen next morning showed that their tools were worn out: chisels sharpened down to the last half-inch, hammers misshapen lumps of steel, nails used to drill holes, flat rocks serving as anvils. Yet these artisans – carpenters, motor mechanics, sheet-metal workers, tailors – were directly improving life in their villages. *They* by the thousands, not the foreign experts, were the real development workers, yet their equipment was badly worn and woefully inadequate. So why didn't they buy new? Shops in Kampala did display imported tools, but they were in short supply, too expensive for village craftspeople and often of poor quality steel.

In tools, Glyn began to see an idea that could inspire an organisation, empower working people overseas, avoid traditional Aid traps and raise crucial questions about world poverty.

---

* A second powerful influence was the philosophy of Fritz Schumacher, as expressed in such works as *Small is Beautiful*. There, he contrasted the energy and creativity to be found in small, democratic groups with the inertia and oppressiveness of large, hierarchical institutions.

He returned home to Gosport, Hampshire, to teach at Portsmouth Polytechnic, but still determined to support African artisans. Many unproductive months went by. Where to obtain tools in quantity? Would companies donate them? Would Government finance a scheme? Fundraising to buy new, in bulk, would be hard. And even if he did strike it rich and buy tools wholesale, how would this 'forge links of understanding' between working people in Britain and rural Africa? Months turned into years, and he was getting nowhere.

One afternoon, his mother, Ruth Roberts, suggested that he make a start by emptying their garden shed of his late father's tools. He sniffed at the very idea. Mothers! He wanted fifty thousand gleaming beauties, razor-sharp, in nice plastic cases, not rusty rubbish from the 1940s. But when they looked them over he had to admit that his father's stuff was in quite good shape. And then Ruth pointed out that in their street there lived '*several other widows and retired working men who would surely let us have what they don't need, rather than see it go to waste*' – and with those words the central concept of TFSR flashed into view.

But would people hand over their tools of a lifetime? Ruth went out, knocked on a few doors and came back smiling. The two of them then did a few sums. On a town plan they counted the number of streets in Gosport, then added estimates for Portsmouth and Southampton. Thousands. Next, what about London, the Midlands, the industrial North? It became astronomical. If their street were anything to go by, they could get millions upon millions of tools, from homes across the land, and all for free!

Glyn didn't sleep that night, as earlier development principles began to connect with the day's marvellous breakthrough. Everything seemed to slot together so naturally, so obviously, that he kept thinking, 'Why didn't we come up with this ages ago?'

Before rushing off to collect tools, though, he knew that two other building blocks were vital for the scheme to succeed: first, a reliable distribution group overseas, with aims and values compatible with his own*, and second, an advisory body in the UK to give the scheme wise counsel and formal backing.

Once again, time passed, but in the summer of 1978 Arthur Gillette, of the

---

* A year or two later I met the social philosopher Ivan Illich - known for his critique of formal institutions in education, health and the professions - and I asked how he would handle distribution. 'Theft,' he replied, 'Just stand them around and let them get stolen.' I objected that people in the UK would find this unacceptable. 'That's your problem,' he replied, 'You asked me the best way to get tools to impoverished people who will really use them, and I've told you.' Hmm. GR.

Youth Division at UNESCO in Paris and an old friend from voluntary service days, asked him to do some research in Tanzania. Now he could look into the first issue: distribution.

In Dar es Salaam he visited the semi-governmental Small Industries Development Organisation (SIDO) and met its energetic and enthusiastic Director, Mr BP Mramba, who immediately spotted the potential of *Tools for Tanzania*, as it was then called. Like Mwalimu Julius Nyerere himself, Mr Mramba knew that artisans in cooperatives and small businesses needed both skills training and quality tools. Indeed, SIDO had earlier trained young artisans and sent them out into the world equipped with tool kits. Rising costs had put a stop to this, though the training courses continued.

SIDO had officers in all regions of the country encouraging craftsmen and women right down to village level and advising them in business methods, design and production techniques. SIDO also agreed to import and store the tools in Dar es Salaam and arrange their free transport to regions inland.

Since Tanzania (unlike Uganda, by then in chaos under Idi Amin) was committed to a fair and equal society, partnership with SIDO seemed ideal.

They promised to draw up a request, detailing numbers and types of equipment needed, and to send it to Gosport by October (they did: it was for 16,000 tools, far more than anticipated) and Glyn came home to focus on the second building block – a committee to guide the growth of the organisation.

Its first meeting took place at 1, Little Anglesey Road, Gosport at 7.30pm on 7th November 1978. Present were Ruth, Glyn, his wife Sigyn and Sarah and Charles Hirom, both long-term activists with the World Development Movement. At a second meeting a week later, Eddie Grimble* joined the team.

They set out their aims and Glyn agreed to act as unpaid Coordinator, to maintain correspondence with SIDO and to rally students at Portsmouth Polytechnic for a first tools collection.

At lunchtime on 14th November, they held a 'Hand-tools meeting' in the TV room of the Students' Union, chaired by the Rev. Peter Wright, the Polytechnic Chaplain. This brought together eight volunteers. Glyn went through the scheme and detailed the huge SIDO request. On 22nd November they distributed the first leaflets in four streets near the Fratton Park football ground, and three days later made the first-ever tools collection. More leafleting

---

* Then a young PhD student, Eddie could little imagine that this meeting was the start of a volunteer commitment (alongside his teaching career as Head of Science) for a full thirty years.

ABOVE **TFSR's first photo. In the Portsmouth workshop (1979)**

followed on 29th November, in Baffins and Farlington (districts of Portsmouth) and they made a second collection.

These first two efforts struck gold* so they needed a Fort Knox in which to store it. Good fortune smiled: on 8th December they got the key to an abandoned church hall (St. Andrew's, now demolished) close by the Portsmouth Guildhall. It had no heating, no water, no gas, no furniture – but they were jubilant. They had a home - somewhere to refurbish their first batch of 300 tools. They made a work bench out of timber from skips, bolted down three vices from their haul and, with little idea of how to refurbish, began to sandpaper those first rusty blades.

---

* If they hadn't – and many subsequent collections were failures – who knows, TFSR might never have come about.

The Early Days

1979 – 1983

DURING THE SPRING OF 1979, Glyn was still lecturing full time at Portsmouth Polytechnic, but twice a month several students, Eddie and he, helped now and then by his young sons and the Hiroms, made street collections around the city. As the pile of tools grew in the workshop they ran weekly refurbishing sessions. It was damp and cold in the unheated church, with just two weak electric bulbs for lighting and no power tools to speed the job along, but they warmed up by sandpapering and wire-brushing. They had to learn basic techniques: how to fix a hammer head securely, what angle to sharpen chisel blades and – trickiest of all – how to sharpen saws. They contacted several elderly craftsmen for tips on refurbishing. Each had years of experience and spoke with great authority, but time and again they gave contradictory advice, so the team was sometimes little the wiser.

In May, Southern TV arranged to come and film one Monday afternoon, but never arrived. Then two days later they turned up at just an hour's notice and Glyn had no time to get his team of regulars together. 'No problem,' said the TV producer, 'ask a few student volunteers to act the part.' Actors were recruited and the producer invited an attractive girl (predictably) to examine a plane close-up to the camera. She did, turning it over and running her thumb along the newly sharpened blade. 'Cut!' called the producer, as deep red blood fountained on to the floor.

By 9th June the Portsmouth group had 1,400 tools – clean, sharp and secure – crated up and ready to ship to Tanzania. It was only a fraction of SIDO's request, but a start. On that day, they organised a small ceremony in the old church hall with a representative from the Tanzanian High Commission in London. He said, 'This is a beautifully simple idea. It cuts through so much of the Aid theory and puts tools into the hands of those who will use them to the benefit of the local community.'

Also present were Frank Judd MP and his wife Chris. Frank spoke, emphasising the value of TFSR as a form of development education in Britain. 'Tools,' he said, 'make a real, tangible connection between our lives here and the lives of working people in the Third World. This is one of the most imaginative ideas I have come across for a long time.'*

---

* Though complimentary, Frank was in no way retracting the challenge he had made several years earlier: 'Start an organisation, and you too will have to make compromises.' His words were to prove prophetic on several occasions.

To a round of applause, the Tanzanian diplomat nailed the lid of one crate (with a 'golden' nail) and a few hours later the full consignment was on its way to Southampton docks. Glyn's old friend Arthur Gillette in Paris had tackled UNESCO and they, somewhat puzzled by his odd request, agreed to pay shipping costs.

This day produced two notable bonuses, quite apart from the boxes leaving for Africa. Chris Judd, wise, friendly and very knowledgeable about the British political scene, agreed to become Chairman of TFSR (she refused to be Chair or Chairperson). Secondly, the Sunday *Observer* ran a short article about the Portsmouth event, with a photo the size of a postage stamp.

The effect was staggering. For several days after the *Observer* article, the postman turned up at Little Anglesey with stacks of letters, perhaps two hundred, from people all over the country. 'How can I help?' they asked, 'How do I organise a collection? What insurance cover will we have against accidents? My garage is available and I have worked with tools all my life. If I start a refurbishing group will you come and give a talk? My husband died recently and left a shed full of tools. Please collect at your earliest convenience.'

It was exciting to get such a response, but it was scary too. The idea was racing away by itself. Almost overnight *Tools for Tanzania* turned from being a small local action into the nationwide *Tools for Self Reliance*, the new name inspired by Nyerere's philosophy and prospects of helping more than a single country. People from Aberystwyth to Ramsgate, Jersey to Newcastle wanted firm details as to transport, insurance, refurbishing... 'Would T-S-F-R* pay petrol costs? Did street collectors need a licence? Who would use the tools overseas? Was it OK to sell antiques? Could worn files be re-sharpened? Would TFSR send some tools to a leprosy colony in India? Did Tanzanians use knitting machines?' The advisory group needed to respond quickly, but didn't know half the answers.

It met several times during mid-1979 to draw up ethical guidelines for helpers collecting tools. For example, once a tool was accepted on the doorstep, it belonged morally to an African artisan, not to the TFSR collector, however much he fancied it, even if he was ready to pay. Nor should tools be sold locally**, not even to raise money for good causes. Why? Because if collectors kept back or sold tools donated for Africa, the press and public would soon make a story out of it.

---

* For some strange reason, many people still persist in calling it 'T-S-F-R' to the present day!

** This high-principled policy, like many others, had later to be modified in the light of practical demands. However, TFSR came up with an acceptable, even ingenious, solution – see page 68

> *Glyn told me of his shipping problem and I found a budget from which the money could come. But when the contract reached the Procurement Officer he refused to approve it because, he sniffily told me, 'UNESCO does not deal in trash!' I went over his head (the kind of bureaucratic step I usually despise) and, on order of his superior, he gave way. The tools went.*
>
> *Later, a group came from TFSR to UNESCO here in Paris, to do an information session about tools recycling and I began to think that we could do something similar. Amongst other items, we furnished free of charge 52 retired Swiss Army minibuses and jeeps to youth projects in places as far-flung as Armenia, the Gambia, Rwanda and Uzbekistan.*
>
> *Some years later, the stubborn Procurement Officer retired and, to my surprise, invited me to his farewell party. Great was my astonishment when, in a goodbye speech, he said (words to this effect), 'In my long career purchasing and supplying schoolbooks, computers and so on to UNESCO field projects – expenditure totalling millions of dollars – I have never derived so much satisfaction as when I was forced to approve the quite modest cost of shipping to Africa some boxes of recycled equipment sent by a British organisation called Tools for Self Reliance.*
>
> ARTHUR GILLETTE, *FORMER HEAD, YOUTH DIVISION, UNESCO*

Many other choices needed to be made about keeping the practical work true to the original ideals and principles. For instance, things had tailed off at the workshop that summer, with the Poly students on vacation. Then International Voluntary Service and the Campaign Against the Arms Trade got in touch. They had people coming to Portsmouth for a week to protest against an arms sales exhibition, but also wanted to use our workshop 'to send tools rather than weapons of destruction to the Third World'. Great: the tools idea linking up with wider issues! And what could be more harmful to Africa's development than the arms trade? But others, more cautious, wondered if TFSR risked criticism for being political, so discussion ensued. Finally, the project went ahead – and went well, with no repercussions.

But back to the organisational side. TFSR had to find out about insurance, the cost of a nationwide scheme, and who/what might such insurance cover? The remainder of the SIDO request had to be shared out between other refurbishing groups, and cheap (or free) ways found to transport tools to the south coast. Feedback from Tanzania was vital to inspire and inform new groups. And the Portsmouth workshop was bursting with tools, with more awaiting collection from Newbury, Ramsgate and Jersey. Suddenly, a host of tasks arose, practical and administrative. Several people were able to volunteer a bit of their time, but who could give continuity, and plan the whole?

As a start, Glyn took six months' leave from the Polytechnic, just to keep things going. This was made possible thanks to support from the Peter Selwood Charitable Trust, Tim Selwood and the Minstead Lodge community in the New Forest, who were soon to play a much bigger role in TFSR's development.

Alongside all these tasks, TFSR itself urgently needed to adopt a formal structure (this should surely have been done sooner). Those who knew, advised going for a standard format, rather than concoct TFSR's own set of statutes. The committee looked at various options – a workers' cooperative, a beneficial society, a membership organisation – but Michael Howson-Green, a helpful Southampton accountant, advised becoming a Limited Liability Company with charitable status. The committee was not too happy with this, mainly because it seemed to offer such limited scope for democratic membership. But Michael said that, surprisingly, a company structure could be less bureaucratic and more flexible than other formats and TFSR could always extend membership once it was safely off the ground. The committee got hold of a standard company constitution, its *Memorandum & Articles of Association*, and was stunned. 'Less bureaucratic? Flexible?' Twenty-two pages; one hundred and eighteen closely typed paragraphs and sub-clauses of legalistic jargon! Already on page one they hit trouble trying to define TFSR's plans to promote solidarity between working people and expose the powers behind world poverty. It turned out that such aims were not acceptable under company or charity law. At best, they could be merely hinted at*. There were dozens more paragraphs to puzzle out and tailor to TFSR's needs, and time and again Frank Judd's prophesy came to mind: 'You too will make compromises'. In the end, they accepted that these

---

* The awful wording finally accepted by the authorities reads: 'Object 3 (2) (d) To promote and encourage research into the causes effects and means of alleviation of all forms of special problems arising from the lack of suitable tools and all forms of poverty and disseminating the results of such research' [sic].

were mostly enabling paragraphs – that would give scope to, rather than limit, the actions of TFSR.

At its meeting in November, the TFSR advisory body resolved to end the uncertainty and register as a company: Tools for Self Reliance Ltd. The first directors – and members – were to be Chris Judd, Arthur Gillette, Sarah Hirom, Glyn Roberts and Peter Gardner of the Minstead Community. Once registered, TFSR would seek charitable status. The directors decided to take out Third Party insurance against claims up to £250,000 and also to announce the first-ever TFSR Gathering, inviting activists from around the country, one weekend in February 1980, to Minstead Lodge in the heart of the New Forest.

By November, two fresh requests for tools had come in: from a cooperative farm in Guinea Bissau and a UN programme for Zimbabwean refugees in Mozambique. In addition, SIDO was still waiting for the 14,600 tools from its original request. Pressures were building, but by now new groups in the UK were taking serious steps to collect tools, and four more refurbishing workshops were being set up besides the one in Portsmouth.

Towards the end of 1979 TFSR published its *Information Bulletin No. 1*, which detailed fifty groups established in England and Wales. Some 'groups' were simply individuals or couples, like Phil and Del Jones in Ramsgate who collected over 1,500 tools between them, without a car of their own. Elsewhere, church-, school-, Rotary-, Lions- and student bodies adopted TFSR. In Bristol, the university Anti-Apartheid association decided to do its bit for the Zimbabwean refugees in Mozambique. *Bulletin No. 1* also showed the TFSR logo for the first time. Glyn had drawn a carpenter, deliberately ambiguous as to whether African or European, male or female, planing a piece of wood, and added two stars to give a revolutionary touch.

The small team in Gosport ended 1979 well pleased with the year's work.

1980: *A good Gathering – but disappointing news from Africa*

Thirty people met at the Minstead Lodge gathering. Most of those already mentioned were there, plus Mark and Sheila Smith*, a representative of SIDO and a married couple from London, Jan and Jackie Hoogendyk, both inspiring people, who were later to play a major part in TFSR. Jan came from a rigidly Calvinist Boer family in South Africa, which had rejected him for his socialist

---

* Mark and Sheila, ex-VSO volunteers in Tanzania, had returned to the UK and rented a flat in Gosport in the summer of 1979. Almost immediately they joined TFSR, collecting and cleaning tools during the autumn, but they also wanted to help the organisation itself to develop.

beliefs back in the 1940s, even before he joined the African National Congress. He was one of the accused at the infamous Treason Trial (1958-1961), along with Nelson Mandela, though always seated next to the Nobel Peace Prize winner Chief Albert Luthuli, as prisoners were marched into the dock each day in strict alphabetical order. After the trial, Jan received a banning order, but he and Jackie evaded the authorities and fled to England.

The Gathering discussed fundamental principles – solidarity rather than charity, the wonderful potential of hand tools in a world of erratic oil prices, the wish to support cooperative efforts overseas and the need to keep TFRS's running costs down. Those present also considered what kind of structure they would like to see in a national organisation. There was a clear wish to keep things simple, with local groups and individuals remaining pretty autonomous. Central TFSR was asked to draft a basic contract to link UK groups and TFSR Ltd. Michael Howson-Green's hunch had been right: people did not want a cumbersome membership organisation. Mr Mlagala of SIDO described the life of village artisans in Tanzania, and Jan Hoogendyk spoke of his dream of TFSR supporting school children who had fled from South Africa to seek refuge in neighbouring countries.

And, of course, everyone refurbished. Thirty people worked round a wide circle of tables, cleaning, sharpening, oiling, swapping tips, and chatting generally. It was an inspiring weekend for all.

April 1980 saw TFSR Ltd. finally registered (Charity recognition took much longer). Glyn was formally appointed Coordinator, and Mark, Hon. Secretary. Directors also opened a bank account, set an accounting date and chose auditors: Michael Howson-Green's firm generously offered its services free. Tedious stuff? Maybe, but essential, if TFSR were to handle finances seriously. And serious finances were needed!

Fundraising has scarcely featured so far, but this was yet another area that needed planning and hard work. The Peter Selwood Trust had made its vital contribution towards the first six months running costs, but could not repeat the grant. Likewise, it was clear that UNESCO would not help again with shipping. Here, Christian Aid saved the day by stepping in, but it was still letter writing non-stop, and Glyn was now back full time at the Polytechnic and could only spend evenings and weekends in the TFSR Head Office (a table in a bedroom at home). June brought welcome news. Thanks to a grant from the Joseph Rowntree Charitable Trust, the directors were able to appoint Sheila Smith as Assistant Coordinator and it was a

THE EARLY DAYS 1979-1983

ABOVE **The first Annual Gathering, Minstead Lodge (1980)**

relief to see new progress on the many tasks in hand. Sheila worked days and Glyn did the night shift, so they didn't see much of each other, but kept in touch through hand-written notes left on the table. The person on whom the strain did fall though, was Sigyn, as her lovely bedroom filled up with boxes, papers, shelves and filing cabinets; and the Roberts' home phone rang day and night since TFSR couldn't afford a separate line.

July saw an innovation: an international voluntary workcamp near Bristol organised by the Quakers and led by Martin Fairbairn, another Gosport friend. Here, for a couple of weeks, 18 young people lived and worked together, had a great time, and refurbished a sizeable pile of tools. This was the first fully-fledged TFSR workcamp and many more were to follow over the years. Nearly all have been successful, some extraordinarily so.

But August brought disappointing news, causing serious concern. In that month, Mark and Sheila and Sarah and

Charles Hirom paid their own way to visit Tanzania and discovered that many of the tools from the first consignment were still lying in the SIDO store in Dar es Salaam. It seemed the Regional Officers, who had direct contact with villages, had not fully understood about TFSR, so few proper requests had come down to Dar es Salaam. And where they had, the storekeeper did not know which tools were needed by carpenters, which by metalworkers, which by mechanics, etc. – and had seemingly given up on the task. This came as a real blow, as everyone had thought that the first consignment was long since in the hands of village people.

Autumn 1980 saw the drafting of two key documents:

a) **Kit lists for UK groups** To avoid the Dar es Salaam bottle-neck, TFSR directors agreed with SIDO to send future consignments in pre-packed boxes, but the UK refurbishing groups (like the hapless SIDO store-keeper) did not know which tools, and how many, should make up a kit. Unfortunately, neither did Sheila nor Glyn; so it all had to be researched, checked out with people skilled in the various trades (tailoring, building, etc) and written up. These lists were later revised many times following feedback from overseas partners, especially once TFSR started to support African blacksmiths in making tools locally.

b) **An Agreement to Cooperate** This was the simple contract, proposed by the Minstead Gathering, outlining the rights and responsibilities of UK groups, TFSR Ltd. and overseas partners. Everything was covered in one three-page document: no legalistic jargon, crystal clear, in contrast to the *Memorandum & Articles of Association.*

As the year drew to an end, TFSR could report sending tools to Tanzania, Guinea Bissau, Angola and Bangladesh, 5,339 in all, bringing the cumulative total to 6,739. Not bad going, considering all the other organisational demands. But a new problem raised its head in the last days of the year: the abandoned Portsmouth church was to be demolished in the spring, so a new workshop had to be found and all the tools and refurbishing equipment shifted.

1981 *From a Bishop's wine cellar to the dog kennels*

As a mature student on a sociology course back in the 1970s, Mrs Joan Russell of Gosport was once asked, unexpectedly, what her lifetime's ambitions were. Off the cuff she replied, 'Save the Old Rectory on Little Anglesey Road from dereliction and – er – do something to help the Third World.' There is no room here for the whole story, but suffice to say that within ten years she had bought and renovated the

THE EARLY DAYS 1979–1983

ABOVE The first workcamp (1980)

fine old Rectory, yet had got nowhere regarding help to the Third World. And so it seemed almost miraculous, certainly marvellous, when this lady – virtually Glyn's next-door neighbour – suddenly offered TFSR the use of her cellars as a workshop and store.

True, they were a bit damp, having been built in 1348 to store wool (exports) and wine (imports) for the Bishop of Winchester. Against this, they were very handy, being close to the office and had the special attraction of being rent-free. In fact Joan even offered to make and sell cream teas in the modern (Georgian) part of her house to generate a small income for TFSR.

Shifting the thousands of tools from Portsmouth to the Old Rectory was a back-breaking job, but eventually each alcove in the Bishop's wine cellar got a new label: **PLANES; HAMMERS; SAWS; DRILLS** and was filled accordingly.

While the Gosport group – basically several families with numerous children – cleaned tools, either below stairs or on the lush Rectory lawn, directors' meetings went on at 1, Little Anglesey.

27

THE EARLY DAYS 1979-1983

> *On assuming the position of Director General of SIDO in 1980, I believed that SIDO-TFSR collaboration offered a special opportunity for practical implementation of Small is Beautiful in Tanzania. I encouraged Regional Managers to seek needy members of village communities who could benefit from TFSR collaboration and submit requests for tools if they felt the need. Requests overwhelmed us. The idea of tools for self reliance was thrilling everyone. There was something special about it, whether it was thirst for self reliance or desire to do away with dependency, or wish to be free from poverty and to be well to do, each applicant knows why, but requests came from all corners of Tanzania. Applicants were based in urban as well as rural areas, individual, groups, cooperatives and village governments. Men and women as well as youths, and elderly sought tools from TFSR. Applicants waited patiently for tool kits to arrive but when it took too long they complained.*
>
> *When the boxes began to arrive in hundreds, we faced many challenges including time consuming process to secure Government exemption for import duty and taxes. SIDO had to approach its parent ministry who, on being convinced of the merits, had to appeal to the Minister for Finance who, if satisfied, instructed Tanzania Revenue Authority accordingly. SIDO lacked in-house capacity to clear the goods from the port, therefore a private clearing and forwarding agent was contracted. This arrangement assisted in reducing the heavy burden of storage*

New refurbishing teams had sprung up around the country, notably in Sheffield, Cambridge and Settle. And some excellent requests had come in, which were readily approved. Two were from Tanzania, but others came from Colombia, Eritrea, Sierra Leone and Ghana.

One Tanzaniaian request came from the African National Congress (ANC), prompted by Jan Hoogendyk, and was for the hundreds of young people at the Solomon Mahlangu Freedom College near Morogoro. These had fled from South Africa after the Sharpeville massacre in 1960 and were in need of adult care and a proper education. The college (named after a young boy shot dead by police in the massacre) had been built by the ANC, helped by many international Anti-Apartheid groups. TFSR was proud to support such a worthwhile cause.

The second request came through the Britain-Tanzania Society, a body with Quaker connections, to help a training centre, the Nkowe Rural Trade School, *and demurrage charges as well as other costs in the port. SIDO-TFSR collaboration presumed duty- and tax-free imports and SIDO's financial capacity to do clearing, forwarding and delivery to Regional Offices and to the ultimate beneficiary. SIDO had no such funds, the Government was reluctant and most clients were not able to bear such costs. SIDO was short of cash but in the end cash was raised, goods cleared and stored in warehouses. As it was, SIDO was really caught between the rock and the hard place!*

Working capital strain experienced at SIDO headquarters was also shared at Regional Offices. What this amounts to is that it took long for some kits to reach original applicants. In some cases original applicants gave up, and with consultation and approval of TFSR the tool kits were reallocated (I am not sure whether we always did this!)

I recall the international tools conference at Arusha, where the late Mwalimu Nyerere and Bishop Trevor Huddleston, alongside retired Prime Minister Hon. John Malecela worked with us for two days. We left Arusha very much-rejuvenated people. We were more convinced than ever that we were on the right track. Tools are a springboard for development, peace, harmony, South-South collaboration, as well as international cooperation.

MR E.B. TOROKA, *FORMER DIRECTOR GENERAL, SIDO, TANZANIA*

in Lindi Region far down in the south of the country. Again, TFSR was pleased to help, and for rather special reasons.

The Quakers (Society of Friends) had been something of an inspiration behind TFSR. Though not a member of the Society, Glyn had volunteered for Quaker workcamps twenty-five years previously. They had been egalitarian, considerate and modest; they made decisions by consensus rather than voting. When there was stress, reconciliation became of first importance. Of course they had fun too, but somehow there was a quiet wisdom about their ways. And they were effective, they really got things done. Glyn was impressed by their approach and years later hoped that TFSR itself could adopt their simplicity, frugality and respect for others.

Another thing. Membership of the Britain-Tanzania Society consisted of *equal numbers* of British and Tanzanians. Impressive! Did any other membership organisation have such a genuine North-South balance? Could TFSR emulate this one day – a membership organisation with equal numbers of people from the North and South?

The Nkowe Trade School gave two-years' training to young men in woodwork, metalwork and masonry, and to young women in domestic science, but it was very short of tools and equipment. For example, on the masonry course, thirty students had *two* trowels between them for bricklaying. And the school didn't even own these. Each morning, a trainee had to run up the hill to the Catholic mission, knock on the door and ask to borrow the mission's trowels. And every evening hand them back.

Directors approved both these requests. 880 tools met the needs of the Freedom College. It closed down some years later, as the South African situation improved and students returned home. The relationship between TFSR and Nkowe (1,500 tools; many more were to follow) was to last for much longer. With other requests, things were not so rosy. In the spring, SIDO reported that 1,163 tools had been delivered to 18 village workshops and two training centres, which was good news, but 4,417 still languished in Dar es Salaam.

And communication seemed to have died with correspondents in Namibia, Guinea Bissau, Laos, Sierra Leone and Zambia. This was before faxes, e-mails and cheap phone calls. TFSR and its overseas partners relied entirely on air mail letters, which often took weeks to arrive, and months (literally) to produce a reply.

And there were other problems. Despite Joan Russell's kindness, the Old Rectory cellars could not cope with all the crates piling in from refurbishing groups around the country. Meanwhile, at 'Head Office' down the road, Sigyn was in despair: truck drivers ringing the doorbell, crates dumped in the front garden, boxes of tools blocking the porch, directors' meetings in the garden, phone ringing, stacks of post to sort and - worst of all - her bedroom still commandeered by TFSR. 'I know you and Sheila do your best to keep it tidy,' she sighed, 'but somehow it doesn't feel like home any more'*.

In July, Sheila and Glyn drafted a paper for the directors, which said that TFSR needed to get its house in order, literally and metaphorically. Without adequate premises, personnel and funding – TFSR might as well shut up shop, or pass over the tools idea to a big, well-organised operation like Oxfam or Christian Aid. Several were contacted, provisionally, but none thought the idea had much of a future.

---

* In fact, Sigyn was the most patient and supportive wife I could ever have hoped for; she backed us 100%. But with three young children to look after, and me fully occupied with the Polytechnic and TFSR, she said that solidarity with the world's poor was fine, but she could do with some, too. GR *

Needing no persuasion on this, directors launched a search for premises large enough to house an office, tools store, refurbishing workshop and an area for crating and dispatch. And since Eddie Grimble had helped to inspire a Youth Opportunities Programme (YOP) tools group in Southampton, itself a port with shipping lines to East Africa, they looked in that direction.

The same meeting settled another matter. One bit of equipment, of which TFSR was always short, yet which was vital to carpenters, furniture makers, metalworkers and builders alike, was the vice. Directors agreed to buy new vices for making up kits, and raise money for their purchase with an appeal. So it was that TFSR came to run its very own Vice Fund.

That summer saw further camps, one at Chapeltown in Leeds, and a Tanzania Solidarity Workcamp at Crowthorne in Berkshire. When not collecting and cleaning tools, the 16 volunteers from eight countries (including two from Tanzania) discussed social and economic conditions in East Africa. Boring? Not at all. They covered culture, art and music with great zest, livened up further by an Open Day with almost 100 visitors, of whom twenty were from Tanzania. Key to the camp's success was a young Oxford undergraduate, Michael Jacobs. He combined intelligence with progressive ideas and good humour, and made a great contribution. The workcamp also opened up a new issue for TFSR – the full and equal participation of people with a disability. Ruth Bailey was wheelchair bound, but played a prominent part in all the camp's activities and left, planning to start up a refurbishing group of her own Lessons learned here were valuable later for TFSR workshops at local and national level. Crowthorne was productive too: The Roberts's little Citroen 2CV sagged low on its springs heading back to Gosport with 800 shining tools.

This well-run camp also had support from the local community, in particular from Dorothy and Chris Cussens, who went on to take a great interest in TFSR generally. Appropriately named from Glyn's point of view, since Dorothy is indeed his cousin, they came to play an important role in the organisation's development. Dot was a director and also Chairperson for several years and dealt with some tricky problems.

Netley Marsh

Noted in Glyn's diary for 24th August, 1981: *Meet Peter Gardner. The Kennels, Netley Marsh. Goodies Fish & Chips on left. Go past into N.M.* A few days earlier, Peter had rung to say that some derelict farm buildings were for sale near Totton, three miles west of Southampton. Well, they were once farm buildings, but had been used for years as kennels for racing greyhounds. When the Southampton dog-track closed, The Kennels became redundant, and were now for sale. £110,000. Could someone from Gosport come and look the place over?

Peter – one of the most enthusiastic, persuasive people it's possible to meet – joined Ruth and Glyn at The Kennels, and they inspected the site. Impressions: On the main road – good. Some three acres of land – very good. A fairly modern semi-detached house – excellent. A huge hangar of a building – what, 100 feet long? – big enough to store any number of tools. Fantastic! And ten other barns, sheds and lean-tos in a sorry state: walls bulging, slates gone, gutters dangling, doors and windows off their hinges. And rats, grown large and fat on dog meal spilled from split sacks, watching placidly from various nooks and crannies.

Every building but the house was packed with concrete or timber stalls, over three hundred of them, bedded with urine-soaked straw, their gates gnawed and scratched by generations of barking greyhounds*. Between the buildings sagged dozens of wire-netting runs, where the dogs were once exercised, and above these stretched a spider's web of wires and cables for intruder alarms, intercoms and broken halogen lamps. In the field behind, rotting bones poked out from nettle beds. Huge bones. Cows? Horses? Altogether a fearsome place.

Fearsome? *It was brilliant!* OK, there was some rot here and there, a bit of work to do, but Peter and Glyn rushed about like schoolboys imagining where the office would be, a system for 'Tools In & Tools Out', a special unit for making up crates, another for sewing-machines. The potential (as the estate agent had insisted) was enormous. And with so many buildings, some could be leased as craft workshops to bring in money. We were onto a winner! Ruth was less sure (she had once renovated a 17th Century farmhouse and knew the pitfalls) but said she was 'ready to be persuaded'.

But could the board of directors be persuaded? For any hope of success, the price had to come down. Peter immediately set about the task. He had heard that the owner of The Kennels, though a hard-nosed businessman, had a generous streak and if he warmed to an idea – especially if you bought him a beer – well, who knows what he might do. Glyn and Peter met him at a pub, bought him a beer and told him of their dreams. When they casually proposed

---

* We later heard from neighbours that the noise could be terrible, as the dogs were starved before racing to make them desperate to catch the hare. Most villagers were only too glad when TFSR bought the place, as they had feared that it might again become a kennels; but a few were nervous that a 'left-wing group' had bought the property.

THE EARLY DAYS 1979–1983

ABOVE **Ruth, Glyn and Peter inspect The Kennels (1981)**

another beer, he winked and declined. 'No,' he said, 'I'm not going to give you the place, if that's what you think. But I do like your plans. I'll tell you what: £77,500, take it or leave it.'

Peter and Glyn looked at each other, nodded, and shook hands on the deal – though they did at least have the sense to make it conditional on getting planning permission. Then the two raced back to The Kennels, into that huge empty hangar and whooped with joy. But it was still not cut and dried. For a start, TFSR hadn't a single penny in the bank towards the purchase.

Once again, Peter was superb. He spoke with a charitable trust, with Michael Howson-Green and then proposed to TFSR directors, meeting

THE EARLY DAYS 1979-1983

> " *It had never occurred to me that you could repair or refurbish tools – and it was really revolutionary, you know, thinking about tools and what a part they play in people's lives – and all the implications it has for questioning the way that we use our resources in developed countries as well as the way scarce resources are used in underdeveloped countries, and through that, making the link between what we've done to cause underdevelopment in poorer countries and also to mis-develop our own lifestyles.*
>
> JUDY BATES *TFSR LIVERPOOL* "

in October 1981, that they take out a bank loan of £85,000*. A charitable trust would pay the first year's interest to give time for a national appeal for funds, for some buildings to be repaired and rents to come in. Over time, money raised would exceed interest charges and other costs. TFSR would have a home of its own, and one day it would own the property outright and be truly self-reliant.

Directors (who had also looked into other, cheaper options) thought long and hard about the proposal: as a Company, responsibility for the loan would fall on each one of them personally. But 'Netley Marsh', as The Kennels were called from then on, seemed such a great opportunity, they decided to go for it and launch a national campaign to raise £100,000 to cover purchase and renovation of the buildings and site. Local TFSR groups around the country were welcome to help, in cash or in kind, but they would not be asked or expected to provide funds.

The year ended with sixty TFSR groups active in the UK and 6,758 tools shipped out, bringing the total to about 13,500. Besides collecting and refurbishing, most groups also tried their hand at raising issues with the public, *development education* as it was called. They did this through public meetings, slide shows and events. Notable among these were programmes in Birmingham, Exeter, Leicester, Portsmouth, Northampton, Southampton, Leeds, Manchester, Bristol and Wokingham – to name but some. TFSR attracted a very wide range of people – church-based groups, students, retired craftsmen, environmental groups, Third World First, Rotarians – with different backgrounds, skills and motivation.

---

* This sounds derisory in 2008, but prices were very different 26 years ago and interest rates were around 12%. The loan equivalent today might be about £450,000.

THE EARLY DAYS 1979-1983

Local groups were becoming interested in TFSR as an organisation too, and starting to question its structure. In the autumn news bulletin for 1981, Mike Hayes of the Bristol group wrote a piece, 'Bored of Directors?' in which he urged that decisions in TFSR should be made in a more open and democratic manner, not confined to a small group of directors. Directors welcomed this in principle, and asked Mike to draw up a detailed proposal.

Meanwhile the TFSR idea had been taken up further afield. In Northern Ireland, Crumlin Road Opportunities, for unemployed young people, gathered and repaired a vast assortment of tools. Aid Tool Australia sent 1,300 tools to islands in the south Pacific. And groups in Sweden, France and the Netherlands were also starting up. All this news, and more, was shared with TFSR groups at a second Annual Gathering in Leicester.

Requests had come in from Dominica, Kenya, St. Lucia, Cameroon, Ghana, Zimbabwe, and Burundi. The Minstead Lodge community generously allowed Peter Gardner time off, three days a week, to develop a renovation strategy for Netley Marsh workshops.

Towards the end of the year, Southampton City Council gave a civic reception for the High Commissioner for Tanzania when he visited the Youth Opportunities (YOP) tools workshop.

It was an enjoyable affair, in no way diminished by the Mayor referring several times in his speech to 'this wonderful effort to help Tasmania'.

1982 *From euphoria to reality: a huge task ahead*

In the early spring, TFSR obtained planning permission from New Forest District Council (Netley Marsh being just within its district, not Southampton) and bought the property. Already by Easter, Quaker workcampers were burning the stinking straw and scores of wooden greyhound pens. Their working equipment was pathetic. On seeing TFSR's only wheelbarrow – a frame with a wheel, but no box – a passing villager rushed off and gave one of his own.

By then, Eddie Grimble had bravely moved from Minstead Lodge on to the site to act for three months on behalf of TFSR, and by late spring, some of the early euphoria had worn off and everyone began to see what an enormous undertaking lay ahead. Nevertheless, local volunteers came out every weekend, breaking up the wire-netting dog runs, dragging a huge and rusting deep-freeze out of one shed (amazingly, it was sold) putting up shelves for tools in each of the concrete dog pens, re-glazing broken windows and much more. A summer workcamp was planned, to get one barn into good enough shape to rent out.

Meanwhile, the directors and Liz Backhouse of Gosport were investigating every possible source of funding, from simple leaflets, to charitable trusts and the London Marathon, even asking the Tanzanian and Zimbabwean High Commissions to support an application to UNESCO.

On top of all this, the regular work of TFSR was just as pressing. Tools were still pouring in at the Old Rectory and Head Office was still buzzing at Little Anglesey. Crates needed packing and lifting on to lorries. Refurbishing groups were demanding better information, good photos, slide-shows, posters... to do their own promotional and educational work. Many were the talks given to Rotary Clubs, schools and churches.

While most of the information and publicity was of a fairly practical nature, TFSR did not shrink from expressing its philosophy too. Its main publicity document at this time was the *TFSR Handbook*, which – besides describing the technical and organisational side of things – devoted seven pages to the principles that lay behind the action.

With help from directors and others, Glyn and Sheila organised a third national gathering, now called the Annual Conference, in Sheffield. TFSR was not a membership organisation, but the conference gave groups the chance to discuss any aspect they wished, from life in Africa (seen from a range of perspectives – usually those of TFSR's early partners and African students living in Britain) to the nitty-gritty of tools work. Already at this gathering, it was clear that local groups fell into two categories. There were those who were happy with the current TFSR set-up and who enjoyed being virtually autonomous; and those who felt that TFSR should now become a fully-fledged membership organisation, with elected directors. As a first step in that direction, directors agreed that any *bona fide* group who wished could nominate up to two members to take part in board meetings.

And then a new problem arose. Mark and Sheila, after being so fully involved since their return from Tanzania in 1979, decided to work again in Africa, in Zimbabwe, leaving in September. Eddie took over from Mark as Hon. Sec* of TFSR.

One of Sheila's last tasks was to interview a cheerful young graduate, Mary Atkinson, to replace her, on a volunteer wage of £25 a week plus accommodation. One sign of progress: Mary would not work from Little Anglesey, but at Netley Marsh, replacing Eddie in the house when he returned to Minstead Lodge.

---

* Company law requires the Honorary Secretary to see that proper procedures are followed in calling Annual General Meetings, taking minutes of directors' meetings and much else. The post is unpaid.

... It is important for people working with TFSR to advance beyond the idea that 'underdevelopment' is an unfortunate state of affairs in far-off foreign lands, an accident of history, something nasty that is today being mopped up thanks to modern technology and economic growth. The fact is, the whole world is under threat of underdevelopment... The ravaging of tropical forests, the destruction of species, soil and marine life... these will affect everybody.

The textile worker in Lancashire, uncertain of a job from week to week, the landless Brazilian in a dusty shanty town... the Tanzanian peasant-carpenter, the factory worker in Leningrad, the decontamination supervisor at an American nuclear plant – they may think they have little in common, with their different cultures, different political regimes, different levels of technical skill. But in fact, whether they recognise it or not, **what they have in common far outweighs their differences***; and the first thing they have in common is their vulnerability...*

Why, with the resources, energy and workforce available, do vast numbers of people go without work... while many others do jobs that 'rot their minds' (Schumacher's phrase)? The answer to this enormous question – Greed is now supported by high-energy technology... The whole process is destructive of the natural environment... and of the quality of life in human communities. We think we are getting more – in fact we are all being impoverished.

By drawing public attention to the shame of **waste** *(and ours is still a very wasteful society), by pointing out the potential of* **tools** *to promote [community] work and values, and by doing something practical to strengthen international* **solidarity***, TOOLS FOR SELF RELIANCE can make its modest contribution towards a safer world...*

FROM THE TFSR HANDBOOK – FIRST PUBLISHED 1981

ABOVE **The main building, Netley Marsh. Concrete dog kennels still used for storing tools (1983)**

An IVS summer workcamp came and went, and groups of weekend volunteers turned up regularly at Netley Marsh, often families with children, grandparents and friends in tow. One elderly couple, friends of Ruth, poked round the site, then pressed £5 into her hand. 'For disinfectant', they whispered and hurried off to the New Forest.

Everyone did their best, but by mid-September it was clear that the well-meaning volunteers had neither the time nor the skills for such a major building project, so TFSR decided to approach the Manpower Services Commission to see if it might run a Community Programme. Under this, 8-10 young unemployed people usually worked on a project for a year to learn various skills, supervised by a qualified builder. It sounded almost too good to be true. TFSR put in an application.

That autumn, Mary was alone (apart from the rats) on that windswept, derelict

THE EARLY DAYS 1979-1983

kept in touch with Gosport by telephone. Directors knew that they must recruit a second Assistant Coordinator as soon as possible, and were delighted when Michael Jacobs (of the Crowthorne workcamp) agreed to take the post in January 1983.

With so much to preoccupy a small team, tools production fell to about 2,500 in 1982 – a real disappointment, but bringing the cumulative total sent overseas to 16,000.

1983 Building work begins – and a bugle call for democracy

Getting a home at Netley Marsh – massive undertaking though it had been – and having Mary and Michael on the spot, helped to create a new dynamism in TFSR.

Previously, when people heard of it, TFSR had been accepted as 'a good idea', but it remained intangible, lacking credibility. Now, the organisation existed in bricks and mortar – a place one could visit, handle the tools, see different aspects of the work and appreciate the effort and friendly enthusiasm of staff and volunteers, young and old**.

site, and a grim time it must have been for her. The house had no heating but an open fireplace*, and the office had just one electric fire. A few local activists met with her from time to time as a Site Management Committee, but Mary was largely on her own, even though she

---

* Later replaced by a Canadian wood-burning stove. Acquired for a song, literally, composed in the TFSR office and then performed to a New Forest stove specialist, to the tune of *Sloop John B*. ('We were down at Netley Marsh/where the working conditions are harsh/Our fingers that night turned white then a terrible mauve/We want a wood-burnin' stove!', etc...). With one really warm room on the premises, morale soared.

** One feature of TFSR was how several generations of a family often joined in – youngsters fetching, carrying and cleaning bricks and tools, parents doing the heavier or trickier jobs, and grandparents making tea, gardening, helping with fundraising and much else.

True, the site looked a sorry mess, with piles of materials left about by local building firms which donated their old bricks, guttering, doors and windows, rather than use the Council dump. But regular workcamps had already brought several buildings to the point where four could be let out – for woodwork, garden machinery, knitting and bicycle repair. Rents were coming in, and the tenants themselves were generating new ideas and activity.

Serious progress on the building side began in August, with the MSC Community Programme: a team of eight (men and women) led by George Marsh. Looking back at old photos now, it is astonishing what they undertook. Some barns were completely stripped of roofs, walls, floors, till they became empty skeletons... and then rebuilt, with new slates, plumbing, drainage, electrics, doors, windows – the lot. And it all had to meet local planning conditions and building standards.

How was this achieved, with such limited financial resources? £20,000 had come in from the national appeal – staff and directors contacting scores of trusts and foundations, a mammoth task – but that had gone towards paying off the bank loan. And in August a further £21,000 was raised from a BBC Week's Good Cause radio appeal by Bishop Trevor Huddleston. This man of great integrity was well known as an Anti-Apartheid campaigner, member of the ANC and close friend of Nelson Mandela and Bishop Desmond Tutu. He had served for years in South Africa and Tanzania, and so knew Mwalimu Julius Nyerere too. With the radio appeal money, the rents coming in and a knack of finding cheap materials and practical help, TFSR kept its nose above water financially. And local well-wishers gave so much: furniture for the house, new materials such as paint from companies, professional assistance from auditors, architects and planners. Once again, Minstead Lodge – not just Peter Gardner, but the community as a whole, the Peter Selwood Charitable Trust and the many contacts they had in the area – helped to solve problem after problem. And all virtually cost free.

TFSR groups also put in many hours of their time. They came from Ipswich, Sheffield, London, Portsmouth, Gosport and Cambridge, for a weekend or the week, breaking down the concrete dog kennels to clear out the hangar building, laying floors, painting, glazing windows and doing a hundred other jobs.

The move towards democracy

1983 was also the year when the 'TFSR democracy debate' came to a head. At the Annual Conference, the Sheffield TFSR group, and others such as Mike Hayes of Bristol had urged TFSR to live up to its declared principles – share power – and become a democratic membership organisation, with directors elected from and by the members.

In their hearts, most directors were in broad agreement with this. They had never felt quite at ease with the decision to become a limited liability company, with themselves the only members. However, it had served its purpose well, allowing TFSR to press on with essentials rather than have overworked staff spend hours producing vast amounts of paper – paper for anyone who thought TFSR was a 'good idea' and sent in an annual donation, perhaps, but did nothing more.

As it was, the directors met when they could (three or four times a year – even then it was hard to find a day that suited everyone), paying their own travel. They made some key decisions, and then left the coordinators to get on with the job. Meanwhile, groups round the country (perhaps just a couple of individuals, maybe a church or school group with its own identity and rules, maybe a 'proper' TFSR group with a dozen members meeting once a week) remained virtually autonomous. They ran things as they liked, so long as they respected TFSR's basic ethical principles. They were self-reliant financially, getting no funds from the centre, but equally not required to make any contributions towards shipping or administration. TFSR had its accounts audited once a year, naturally, but could not pay professionals to audit the accounts of another 45 groups.

There was also the question of Netley Marsh and the, by now, £65,000 bank loan. The first five directors, who knew and trusted each other, had taken personal responsibility to see that loan repaid and wanted to see the job through. Peter Gardner felt especially strongly that TFSR should not 'open up' until the debt was cleared.

Nevertheless, the times they were a-changin'. Directors met in March, July and November, and called the fourth Annual Conference at Netley Marsh in September – in that great hangar of a building, with 45 people taking part. A major theme of these meetings was the opening up of TFSR to become a membership organisation. (A minor theme of the conference itself was how to keep three boisterous goats, supposed to be tethered in the back field, from wandering in and disrupting proceedings.)

In the light of all these discussions, large sections of the *Articles of Association* were amended – a complicated and time-consuming job. The result was that TFSR remained a company, but broadened out to allow up to 500 members to join. Seven directors would be elected from these, serving three years each, but at staggered intervals, so there would always be some old hands who knew the ropes and some new blood to bring in fresh ideas.

However, most directors still wanted to limit membership to people who were genuinely active with TFSR – collecting or refurbishing tools or doing development education work on the organisation's behalf. The membership fee was set at only f.1; but donating money alone would not entitle someone to membership. Within a year, members of TFSR numbered 44, and they were indeed the activists. TFSR also sought members from its contacts overseas, people who distributed tools or put them to use in the villages. This proved enormously hard to achieve, but there were some notable successes.

Education and evaluation

In the spring of 1983, Michael Jacobs worked late nights drafting a proposal to the EEC (now the European Union) for a two-year development education programme for TFSR, and sent it off with fingers crossed. Then in July, Glyn made a field trip to Tanzania and Zimbabwe, thanks to a grant from the Nuffield Foundation. He came back with a film, photos and some useful findings, among them:

- SIDO staff, and contacts in Zimbabwe, and village craftspeople had essentially no idea where their tools came from, or what TFSR's motives were in sending them. This needed addressing.

- Tool boxes were still sitting in various stores for long periods uncollected. TFSR should stencil the actual village destination on each crate.

- African blacksmiths had a long tradition of making tools, albeit limited in range and design. In collaboration with SIDO and the Zimbabwe Project, TFSR should provide equipment such as anvils, and stimulate the production of a greater range of tools and tool parts (e.g. plane blades), by giving designs and training.

- Tanzanian smiths were desperately short of good quality steel. TFSR could help by sending them the scrap leaf springs of vehicles.

Glyn also came back to some great news – TFSR's EEC application for a development education programme had been approved. On a personal level this gave him a problem. He had always dreamed of working full-time for TFSR, and the EEC project gave him the chance to quit the academic world and join the team. But TFSR could not pay much more than half a Polytechnic salary. With a wife, three children and a mortgage, was it fair to gamble a safe academic post against a chancy two-year contract? Sigyn and Glyn talked long into the night, several nights, and with great courage she agreed to the move. 'We'll get by,' she said, in her lovely Swedish lilt. It made life harder for them in some ways, but at least they had their bedroom back.

In November, Glyn joined the Netley Marsh office in the dual role of Coordinator and Development Education worker, shortly after Shalin Jethi had been employed on volunteer terms to help with the educational work.

The four staff spent many hours that winter shivering in one of the outbuildings which served as an office, and warming up in study seminars at an overheated Southampton University – all with the aim of working out six principal themes on which to hook the TFSR educational programme. The key point remained – that TFSR must be to more than a campaign to ship out quantities of tools, useful though they might be.

The six themes were:
WASTE Obvious connections with tools dumped in Britain, while little is wasted in Africa. Included a focus on life-styles and consumerism

SELF RELIANCE Not competitive individualism that begins and ends with the self, but the cooperative, collective self-reliance of communities

TECHNOLOGY Connections with tools and the power to control production, but also looking at how production and technology can in their turn control people

PARTICIPATION Decision-making; who shall have a say in it?

WORK & LEARNING What are the alternatives to 'mind-rotting' (to quote Schumacher) jobs and enforced 'leisure'? How can the young and unemployed acquire the skills they need for work?

SOLIDARITY More than an empty political slogan. For TFSR it meant practical, politically aware cooperation between communities North and South.

And so another busy year drew to an end, but it had been productive and exciting, with 62 active groups collecting and refurbishing in the UK*, and 9,564 tools sent overseas – to Nkowe, SIDO, Burundi, Zimbabwe, Gambia and Cameroon – bringing the cumulative total to 25,550. And the loan on Netley Marsh was down to £35,000.

---

* Prominent among them were the Garvald Centre in Edinburgh, with Paul Turner; the Sheffield groups with Pedro Conner, Roger Rees and David Griffiths; the Gosport group, with Ian and Liz Backhouse; Settle, Yorkshire, with Kevin Petrie; and Isle of Wight, with John and Judith Fulford.

The Crisis Years
1984 – April 1986

ALTHOUGH THE NUMBER OF TFSR groups increased to 67 in 1984, many were running into problems with premises, volunteer drop-out, and transport of tools to Netley Marsh, from which most shipments left. And on the shipping side, things certainly picked up. During the year, twenty-six consignments (14,173 tools) went on their way, paid for by Christian Aid. This brought the running total to 41,619, sent to 25 different countries. SIDO was the main destination, for almost 6,000, with 1,500 going to agricultural cooperatives in Mozambique, 1,114 to the Nkowe Rural Trade School and 1,536 to the Organisation of Rural Associations for Progress in Zimbabwe (ORAP).

ORAP was an inspiring partner, stimulating village communities to action in the fields of public health, nutrition, child care, water and animal husbandry. Nothing unusual in that, one might think, but it was the way they went about it that was so special. They had a clear philosophy and mature, impressive people leading the organisation by example and informed discussion – TFSR could learn a lot from them. When asked the question of whether tools should be shipped to land-locked Zimbabwe, via the apartheid regime in South Africa or through war-torn Mozambique. Sithembiso Nyoni, a founder member of ORAP, replied,

'We need the tools! Anything sent via Mozambique is likely to be destroyed before it gets here. BUT […] send them via South Africa only on condition that your groups understand our vulnerability and the struggles that we are going through […] as weak villagers. We would expect your groups to do all possible to help us remove this obstacle to the development of the African continent, the […] policy of apartheid. Even at this village level we understand the importance and the role of international links with South Africa and how, in turn, these links jeopardise our position as the weakest in the link.'

The development education programme was evolving too. Staff and directors spent the early part of the year devising a strategy and the later months in giving talks, slide shows, video presentations, games and simulations, on over 100 occasions. They even gave six public talks at the Victoria and Albert Museum, as part of the museum's exhibition of hand tools. On display was a bronze plane from ancient Rome, ornate with the head of Jupiter, but essentially the same tool that any joiner would use today. Another plane, of wood and short as a man's thumb, had served for violin making in the 18th century. Both were thought provoking – of the work of modern artisans and that of craftsmen long ago. (Antonio Stradivari himself proved that the finest quality instruments could be fashioned using fairly basic equipment.)

Site problems

Back at Netley Marsh, work started on a permanent exhibition, not merely photos, but practical displays, to highlight TFSR's six educational themes.

However, workshop renovation progress slowed down agonisingly during the summer of 1984 and early 1985. One Community Programme building team finished, leaving much work still to do, and it took time to recruit another. When that did arrive, its output was, to say the least, sporadic. Supervised, they did deliver the goods, but when George was on other business, work ground to a halt and tea breaks got longer and longer. Materials and expert advice promised from various quarters failed to arrive. Outdoors looked much like a bomb site, and workshop tenants, customers and visitors had to pick their way between open trenches, piles of bricks, roofing slates and timber in the muddy, ill-lit courtyards.

At least Anne Moorshead brightened things up by painting a colourful, 100 foot-long mural on the front wall of the main building. There was much debate over symbolic themes for this – a village, a ship, a bridge, perhaps, linking communities in the North and the South? Staff finally chose a range of occupations with the tools each craftsperson would use. To test a theory, Anne painted only with black, white, red and yellow – no blue. She assured everyone that these colours leave one with a recollection of blue, even though it is absent. Visitors can judge for themselves on this, but the mural as a whole is very striking and still graces the wall today.

But a colourful mural could not lessen the various tensions developing around the site. These grew from the number and variety of people who were now working or living – officially or unofficially – on site. They were often very articulate, with their own philosophical take on the evils of hierarchy* and capitalism, and TFSR staff mostly had similar views. However, it was reaching a point where rents were left uncollected, building work was not progressing and the staff seemed unable or unwilling to put their foot down because exercising authority was considered in some way undemocratic.

A Site Users' Committee had been set up with representatives of staff, tenants, volunteers and outside advisers to deal with such problems, but it fairly soon proposed a way forward that the directors and, indeed, a number of tenants could not accept.

---

*Several gleefully quoted me passages from my own booklet, *Questioning Development*, in which I had distinguished between 'democratic' and hierarchical 'authoritarian' forms of leadership. GR

The main difference of opinion was with those who wished Netley Marsh workshops to run along cooperative lines. It would be a craft centre financially integrated with TFSR, to such an extent that some tenants might no longer pay economic rents but could contribute in other ways. At its most ambitious, it visualised that TFSR would be responsible for selling the craft centre products and would benefit from any profits. The reasoning behind this was that it fitted in with TFSR's stated philosophy of sharing power with the poor and powerless.

The counter-argument, put by the directors and others who did not share this vision, was that a balance must be struck between idealism and pragmatism. (What was it Frank Judd had said?) TFSR bought Netley Marsh for a specific purpose, as a resource for TFSR. The bank loan still needed paying off. Staff had plenty on their hands without trying to run a craft centre. The workshops were for tenants who could pay their way, and rents could not be waived because they had fine ideals and times were hard. Also, some tenants did not wish to be part of a cooperative; they were doing very well, thank you.

I was initially attracted to Tools because I don't like waste – I was interested in recycling. But since I've been involved, I've been interested in development education and I think that Tools is a brilliant 'tool', especially to get kids interested, because anyone likes to pick up a plane and look at it. So I like to use that as a vehicle to talk about broader issues.

ALISON 'JELLIE' CLARKE
TFSR LIVERPOOL

These arguments picked up on the wider debate about democracy. The Site Users' Committee felt that directors were not living up to TFSR's stated principles, while directors felt that they, not the site users, represented the wider TFSR membership and should make key decisions. Also, there was perhaps a view that the Site Users' Committee had lost its grip, encouraging – or at least allowing – anyone to drift in, sleep in unused barns and lead an alternative lifestyle*. At times,

---

*'Fred' (not his real name), who kept chickens on the back field, was much in love with one of our staff, though she did not return his affections. One morning, I was summoned to the yard to find Fred in tears, wringing the necks of his hens and hurling them, one by one, through her open bedroom window. And there was 'Slim', who, to be fair, was always calm and courteous, but could still give us the shivers with his steady, penetrating gaze. We all knew that he kept in his caravan a full set of slaughterer's knives, honed for immediate use should he ever again take up his old job in an abattoir. This is not to say that such characters were a major worry. Most made genuinely useful, if sporadic, contributions. GR

some observers felt, the place resembled a hippie commune rather than the national centre of a responsible registered charity.

To cut a long story short, in late 1984 and early 1985, directors reduced rents by 5-10% in view of the unfinished building work, introduced tighter rules for the use of the Netley Marsh house, and drew up much clearer roles for staff. In particular, Glyn was made sole Coordinator, authorised to take and implement decisions on behalf of the members and directors with respect to the day-to-day administration of TFSR. This did not go down well. The Site Users' Committee protested in a letter to the directors, but got nowhere with it and resigned *en bloc*. Yet despite the new 'fascist regime', which, for a while, was regarded on site as a betrayal of TFSR's finest ideals, working relationships between staff remained generally cordial. There was so much to do; they had to get on with things.

By this time, founding directors Arthur Gillette and Peter Gardner had retired from the Board, to be replaced by Jan Hoogendyk (London) and Roger Rees (Sheffield). Both had strong views about the way TFSR should be going – Jan seeking more support for radical groups in southern Africa, and Roger wanting a more professional approach to administration and finances. In particular, Roger felt the Netley Marsh site was a growing liability to TFSR, in view of its poor state and south coast location. He wanted to see a new, regionalised structure for the organisation.

The new Community Programme building team included a bookkeeper to handle its finances. Her name was Mary Tolfree and, to be frank, she found TFSR the oddest place she had ever worked, with its lofty principles and endless discussions. Basically, she thought everyone else was mad. By the same token, staff thought that an accountant must, by definition, be tedious and pedantic. How wrong on all counts! As the months went by, Mary began to discover a new world beyond her pages of credits and debits, a world she had never come across in a fairly conventional upbringing. And other staff found that she had a mercurial personality, great drive and a deep loyalty to TFSR.

Also new to the staff during the year was Nick Hutchinson, who ran a national 'Sponsor-a-tool' campaign at 21 centres round the country (another of Peter Gardner's bright ideas). It raised £4,000 and thousands of refurbished tools. But there were departures, too – Michael Jacobs moved on to pastures new in August, and Mary Atkinson left at Christmas. Shalin Jethi, who had suffered considerably from ill health, also left that autumn. Suddenly there was a staffing crisis. The posts were advertised – at £30.25 a week, still very

I joined TFSR because it was near where I lived, not from any great desire to change the world. With two toddlers I was just pleased to get a job where they were welcome, or at least tolerated.

Having grown up in an ex-army, very Conservative household and trained in the City to be a Chartered Accountant I was confronted with an environment I found hard, at first, to comprehend. There was no hierarchy, we all mucked in with whatever needed doing and we all had a common goal... though it took me a while to work out what it was.

The work was quite a challenge as I tried to make sense of the accounting records handed on to me, written in pencil in an exercise book and a petty cash box consisting of a jam-jar. An old Gestetner printed inky documents and newsletters, but photocopying meant a two-mile bus trip to the volunteer bureau in Totton.

TFSR was about people in those early years. It must be against the law of averages to come across such a diverse group of extraordinary people within one organization. It is really through them I learned to see the world through different eyes. TFSR also attracted the weird, the wonderful and the downright bloody awful. Among the volunteers we had a murderer, drug addicts, alcoholics, manic-depressives, a child molester, the oldest person in Britain with Downs Syndrome (wonderful Kenny), the product of a sibling union... and a German who insisted vegetables felt pain. Each one was a valuable member of the team.

MARY TOLFREE

much a volunteer rate – plus a room in the house.

On the construction side, the team decided to erect a second floor within the main TFSR building, to provide offices, a workshop and a development education exhibition. The huge attraction of this idea, besides the extra floor-space, was that all three rooms could be heated. Up till then, tool refurbishers and office staff still worked in hats and coats during the winter months, only warming up by the wood-burning stove when they ate lunch in the house each day. A wonderful acquisition in the tools workshop was a horizontal grindstone, which gave chisels a perfectly flat bevel, and saw-sharpening, setting and re-toothing

machines*, which did away with the hardest and most time-consuming of all refurbishing jobs. Two volunteers, Oliver Brooke and Brian Summerfield became specialist saw doctors and re-toothed, set and sharpened some 8,000 saws in their time!

For the second storey, workcampers from Ipswich TFSR dug the footings while the Community Programme lads built the interior walls. And dozens of massive timber joists were bought for next to nothing (new,

ABOVE Dog kennels demolished, prior to raising 2nd floor (1983)

they would have cost a fortune) from the Rank Flour Mills being demolished just then in Southampton. The only drawback, literally, of this precious haul was the hundreds of bent rusty nails to be yanked out before each joist could be put in place.

A welcome addition to the Netley Marsh team around this time was Peter McDermott, who offered his services,

---

*These were donated by Bitterne & Woolston Rotary, one of scores of Rotary clubs to help TFSR over the years. Their efforts at collecting tools, and providing funds and equipment were tremendous, and greatly appreciated, but I sometimes wondered just what they made of TFSR's solidarity message. Did they just turn a blind eye to it, or did some of them quietly agree with us? GR

full-time and voluntarily for the first year. As Peter had taught in Ghana and Kenya, enjoyed design and was very practical, he took responsibility for the new exhibition.

On December 10th 1984, TFSR loaded its first-ever shipping container. It took 14,000kg of scrap steel for SIDO-backed blacksmith groups, and 5,500 tools packed into kits. Loading a container was always hard work, but also fun, and helpers would turn up from miles around, often families – such as Ian and Liz Backhouse of Gosport TFSR and their two boys – and everyone would lend a hand, sharing fruit and sandwiches at lunch time.

For the first few containers, TFSR had no proper lifting equipment beyond an antique, mobile hand crane, which later ended up in a museum. The boxes were unforgiving and extremely heavy, but with good fortune and good management, no serious accident ever occurred. SIDO later thanked TFSR for its 'untiring efforts' with this first container, which was kind of them, though in fact, the efforts had been far from untiring. Loading and stacking 17 tons of wood and steel by hand in a day stretched everyone to the limit.

1985 *The gathering storm*

By this time, TFSR was regularly organising three different sorts of gathering:

a) **The Annual Conference** – a weekend get-together for anyone in TFSR, visitors welcome, where local groups could report on their year's work, discuss the future and enjoy socialising. As far as possible, this Conference moved about, one year in the north, then the Midlands, then in the south… to make travel easier for people.

b) **The Annual General Meeting** (AGM) – legally required under the Articles of Association. At this day long meeting, TFSR members scrutinised the annual report and financial accounts, elected new directors and proposed and voted on any motions to decide policy. These motions could be on any subject, from dropping the 'Ltd.' after the name Tools for Self Reliance (which happened) – to selling off the Netley Marsh site, lock, stock and barrel (which didn't).

c) **Directors' meetings** – were held several times a year, up and down the country. They were for directors, but any member could attend, or receive minutes if they wished (though reports also appeared in the news bulletin, *Elbow Grease*). Directors approved or rejected requests for tools, hired staff, oversaw finances, and generally ensured that TFSR kept to its programme from one AGM to the next and stayed within the law.

At the 1985 Annual General Meeting in Groby, Leicestershire, Glyn resigned as a director as he was employed as Coordinator, and Ian Backhouse joined the Board. Soon after this, Roger Rees took over from Chris Judd as Chairman. It was felt that clearer criteria were needed with which to judge between requests coming in for tools. All could not be approved – they were far too numerous – so the directors needed proper grounds for each decision. They decided to support:

- Groups of craftsmen and women, before individuals
- Indigenous initiatives, rather than 'foreign aid' projects
- The cooperative ethic, rather than competitive business
- Productive units, rather than schools and colleges
- Workers making articles for local use, rather than for sale to tourists, etc.
- Countries with no steel or tool industry of their own
- Initiatives in countries which themselves showed by their development policies a commitment to their poor and rural people.

Roger then produced 16 procedures for the more efficient running of directors' meetings. For a start, each issue would be formulated as a motion and voted on. This was a novelty, but directors thought it would perhaps make for clearer-cut decisions. Next, staff present were no longer permitted to speak unless invited to do so by the Chairman. This felt very strange, as everyone had joined in before without needing formal permission. With some hesitation, for in the past, matters had mostly been decided by general discussion and consensus, directors accepted these procedures, and a new style of TFSR management began.

A little while later, Roger visited Netley Marsh to look over the bookkeeping and accounting procedures, employment contracts for staff, and other contractual and recording systems – and considered many not fit for purpose, where they existed at all. Some were indeed over-simple, having been drafted off-the-cuff, according to the needs and resources of the time. Roger went home to write out new terms of employment for staff modelled on standard documents used by local authorities, trades unions and other such bodies.

In the summer of 1985 TFSR had still only four staff members. Mary Tolfree handled finances, Peter McDermott and Glyn covered a broad sweep of administrative tasks, with Peter specialising in educational materials and Glyn seeing to the organisation as a whole. Finally, David Crawford joined as liaison worker, linking groups in Britain with partners overseas. A young German also gave a hand. As his alternative to military service, Peter Effenburger grappled with the tools store – sorting, shifting, stacking – a heroic task for one person. He was the first of a line of German conscientious objectors, and every one of them was excellent. Peter had some unusual views on life, the universe and everything. He loved painting large, colourful flowers on the TFSR crates before they left. A few people said it made them look unprofessional, but most found them delightful*.

One particular problem in the tools store was the ramshackle shelving, cobbled together from planks and pieces of furniture. It looked a mess and defied any proper storage system. Then one Monday a message arrived: 'The Sellotape factory in Harrow is full of superb metal shelving. Go any day up to Friday and you can take as much as you like. On Saturday, the bulldozers move in and it will be crushed.' The TFSR team hired a flatbed truck, raced to Harrow and unbolted as many 10' high shelf units as possible. Back at Netley Marsh they spent days rebuilding them in the workshop, using hundreds of brackets and thousands of nuts and bolts. Fingers were red-raw, but the end result was very smart and it seemed unlikely that those rows and rows of empty shelves would ever be filled**.

From the earliest days, accommodation for workcampers at Netley Marsh had been primitive, but in 1985 New Forest District Council gave planning permission to erect a bunkhouse. This was all very well, but a second-hand Portacabin would cost about £1,000. Within two days, a letter arrived – completely out of the blue – from the Theosophical Order of Service with a cheque for £1,000. These serendipities seemed to happen again and again as TFSR became more widely known.

The tools idea was now established in Denmark and Holland. In September, Jan Hoogendyk and Glyn went to Amsterdam to take part in a Festival of Tools run by *Gered Gereedschap* ('Used Equipment'). They found the Dutch team cutting out huge replicas – hammers, spanners, axes, 6' long or more – from sheets of thick polystyrene. Late that night they drove into the city centre with the models and balls of string, and the good folk of Amsterdam awoke next morning to find ten of their principal statues superbly attired – Queen Juliana sawing away, Prince Bertil raising aloft a mighty hammer. The newspapers loved it and TFSR learnt a new publicity stunt.

And TFSR itself had something to celebrate. On October 18th, supporters

---

*Once, when a consignment of tools was lost for months in Dar es Salaam, and the port authority denied any knowledge of it, an envoy from Netley Marsh finally spotted Peter's floral boxes in their warehouse – a flourish of reds, yellows and greens in among all the standard crates.

**Of course they were! Soon, every shelf in that large building was stacked high. To the left, shelves were piled with unrefurbished tools, by category. The right hand side was a mirror image of the left – but all clean, sharp, secure and oiled, ready for packing into kits.

gathered at Netley Marsh to witness the ceremonial send-off of the 50,000th tool for self reliance. Representatives of New Forest District Council, Melvyn and Sue Fielding from Blackpool TFSR, helpers from Ipswich TFSR, Rotary, and others saw Richard Jones pack a fine plane for the Weya Cooperative in Zimbabwe. In a short address, Glyn emphasised that while Netley Marsh was the shipping point, the real credit for this achievement must go to local groups all over the country.

On 17th November, with help from Sheffield TFSR, Terry Waite made a BBC Week's Good Cause Appeal for TFSR on Yorkshire TV, and once again several volunteers came in to help with the response. It was exciting to open each envelope, not knowing whether it would contain a £5 note or maybe a cheque for £500. The appeal raised nearly £25,000 and every donor was thanked.

More trouble

Although TFSR was making good progress on some fronts – finances improving, the Netley Marsh site looking better, craft workshop rents coming in, the development education programme creating useful materials and displays – new tensions were emerging between staff and directors, and between directors themselves.

The first tension concerned Netley Marsh and some local groups.

While many groups had helped to refurbish the New Forest site and buildings, and were happy with the loose national structure of TFSR, three directors (Roger Rees and David Griffiths of Sheffield, and Duncan Kerr of Ipswich) felt that Netley Marsh was a huge distraction from TFSR's real purpose. They pointed out that tools production had faltered, while funds and effort – which could have been used for educational work – were going into construction. They also felt that the headquarters were wrongly situated so far south, even though close to a major port.

They therefore proposed to restructure the organisation to cover six regions, from the South West up to Scotland. Each region would own a workshop and employ a properly salaried regional organiser. In addition, there would be a geographically central office with two or three more salaried staff. Such a set-up, they said, would encourage tools and skills exchange between local groups. Regional identities would develop, leading to more democratic representation on the board of directors. A region could take on specific requests and local groups' kits would accumulate at the regional workshops for transport to central office, or perhaps be shipped overseas direct.

The other three directors (Chris Judd, Jan Hoogendyk and Ian Backhouse) opposed this proposal. They felt that selling off Netley Marsh at this crucial point in its development would be disastrous. Even

ABOVE Festival of Tools, Amsterdam. Jan Hoogendyk far right. (1985)

if basic repairs were nearly completed*, it still needed smartening up, especially the unsurfaced courtyards which really let the place down. Selling up would never raise the sums needed to buy six regional premises and a new national centre, let alone pay for nine salaried staff. And to sell off would be to jettison the many thousands of hours of volunteer work that people had put in, and betray the promises of fundraising campaigns over the previous four years. 'By all means let's encourage regional development,' they argued, 'but don't quit now. Having got this far, at least give the place a year or two to deliver on what we've promised.'

But the division went deeper than this. To some extent it arose from a clash of personality and approach, as personified by Glyn and Roger. These two styles are perhaps typical of the stages through which many organisations evolve, large and small.

* In 1987, at Eddie Grimble's suggestion, a private building firm completed the structural work, volunteers tidied up the site, and it was soon an attractive place to work in and visit. Three interest-free loans from TFSR supporters made this possible.

Glyn – along with pioneers like Peter Gardner, Jan Hoogendyk and several others who had started local TFSR groups around the country – was an enthusiast, an initiator. He could get people to share the vision, join in, get a huge amount done, and feel good about it. But he believed that this spirit depended on the team being a happy one, with lightness of touch a key to the administrative side. He knew that the volunteer spirit resists being bossed around. He wanted 'participative democracy' (though even he had had to fall back on the legal authority of the directors when things got out of hand with the Site Users' Committee a couple of years earlier). With the exception of the wordy *Memorandum & Articles of Association*, seldom referred to, most TFSR paperwork was friendly, informal, illustrated and short. Even the financial statements were fairly basic (yet complex, as Mary had to detail accounts for the European Community and Manpower Services Commission, besides TFSR's ordinary income and expenditure) though they remained quite acceptable to the auditors.

This approach is typical of the youthful stage of an organisation, when it is still small and optimistic, and just about everybody knows everyone else.

Roger, on the other hand, was versed in representative democracy and came from a different tradition, rooted in trades union or party-political hierarchy, typical of large organisations, where confrontation is normal, documents are legalistic, and delegates (representing sub-groups) debate, vote to reach majority decisions and negotiate with employers. Skill in negotiation is important, as is knowing and abiding by procedures, and once a decision is made, line management takes over to ensure that it is carried out. This is the way most institutions work, and most such bodies keep their staff engaged, though not always happily so, by paying them normal salaries.

On visiting Netley Marsh in 1985, Roger had been taken aback by its rather amateurish procedures and documents, and decided to draft alternatives. Some of his criticisms were welcomed. The annual reports and quarterly newsletter, *Elbow Grease*, could indeed be more informative and attractive. But other changes were less well received. He considered meetings too lax and unprofessional, 'directors should take their legal responsibilities more seriously' and 'staff should follow decisions more closely and correctly.' These changes were imperative, he claimed, in view of 'the over-riding need to establish a bureaucratic institution as a basis for sound future national growth'.

It was certainly a sober way of doing things, and might well have been

ABOVE **Richard Jones packs the 50,000th tool in front of the mural (1985)**

appropriate if TFSR aimed to become a large professional organisation. But half the directors and all the staff felt very uneasy. The new documents, when they appeared, were long and detailed. *Terms & Conditions of Employment, Complaints and Appeals Procedures,* for example, ran to several pages of typescript. Fine for a post with Shell or a local authority, but off-putting when trying to persuade a young person to take on a job at £32.50 a week.

Believing that 'Small is Beautiful', Chris, Jan and Ian and the Netley Marsh staff were not sure that they, or members generally, *wanted* TFSR to expand into a bureaucratic institution Improvements could be made, certainly, but a turgid bureaucracy would kill the spirit and enthusiasm that people loved about TFSR. And as Glyn in some ways embodied that spirit, they supported him to see through the Five-Year Plan on which directors were currently working.

The first clash came in early January 1986, at a directors' meeting to discuss

> *I like the idea of small-scale, collective, democratic forms of organisation like a Tools for Self Reliance group or a Ujamaa village. I like the idea of recycling. I like the idea of direct practical aid. But also I think that it is a drop in the ocean really – when you think about the vast amount of money that is coming back to the North of the planet in the form of debt repayments every year – the amount we are sending out in terms of tools is very small.*
>
> **PEDRO CONNER** *TFSR SHEFFIELD*

the Five Year Plan. Members of staff were excluded from the first half of the meeting and a long discussion ensued on future staff roles and Glyn's position. Predictably, the three directors who appreciated 'lightness of touch' for TFSR, saw him as a key figure in its future, while those who wanted to sell off Netley Marsh and expand regionally viewed him as the main obstacle.

January to March were generally unhappy months. A couple more directors' meetings made little progress as the two camps jockeyed for position. Everybody knew that matters would come to a head at the Annual General Meeting in April.

As the AGM drew closer, tensions grew. The whole of TFSR heard of the split and a standard visit by Netley Marsh staff to groups in the north drew protests from some directors, that they were canvassing support. A paper written by Duncan Kerr criticised Netley Marsh and proposed that the AGM should consider its sale. This spurred Ian Backhouse to write a counter-proposal detailing its advantages, financial and organisational. He circulated this to TFSR members, urging them to attend the AGM and vote to keep the property. The response from Roger was a furious ten-page 'Open Letter to Ian Backhouse', mailed to all members.

To cool tempers (recalling that Quaker spirit) Glyn wrote to those coming to the AGM, outlined how and why Netley Marsh had been bought, and urged all to consider things in a calm and courteous manner. 'I believe that the *manner* in which we address each other is extremely important,' he wrote […] 'confrontation and the attacking of personalities should be alien to TFSR.'

For all these fine sentiments, the Annual General Meeting, held at the Africa Centre, Covent Garden, on 5th April and chaired admirably by Michael Jacobs who had left his sick bed to attend, was a nerve-wracking affair. But it was carried through in a competent and civilised manner – with some heckling now and then during the motions for and against the sale of Netley Marsh, but that was fair enough. In the event, the proposal to sell was overwhelmingly defeated and new directors were elected who favoured keeping it. The AGM did agree, though, to commission an independent appraisal of different organisational models involving Netley Marsh and the regions.

Despite the clash at the AGM, the new directors recognised that the other camp had put forward many valid points. TFSR did need to improve its systems, including tools-freight around the country. Contracts should be better worded to fulfil legal obligations. Publications could be more professional. Regional development was certainly something to aim for. But they dropped the 16 procedures for meetings and went back to the earlier friendly way of running things – though voting when necessary.

The new board of directors (Chris Judd, Ian Backhouse, Kevin Petrie, Dorothy Cussens, David Nicholson and Jan Hoogendyk) elected Jan as Chairman, and an inspiration he proved to be with his wisdom, humanity, youthful enthusiasm (though he was over seventy) and his wide range of international contacts.

The three disappointed ex-directors resigned from TFSR, and two groups (Newcastle and East Anglia) broke away to call themselves 'Tool Aid'*, but otherwise the hurt feelings and tensions of the previous two years soon faded. The Sheffield group actually stayed within TFSR, much as a result of the mediating efforts of one of its founder members, Pedro Conner. Pedro later played a key part in setting up a network for the freight of tools, and employing a TFSR regional worker for the north.

Directors and staff were a team again, ready to look forward, despite the retirement of Chris Judd, after so many years of friendly guidance. Robin Cluley, an Anglo-Swedish engineer, became workshop organiser at Netley Marsh. Marie Watts, brought calm and flowers to the house, tools store and gardens. Romance blossomed too – Robin and Marie's was TFSR's first wedding, though not its last.

---

* What's in a name? A chosen name says a lot – sometimes misleadingly so. *Aid Tools Australia* suggests a nationalism and 'foreign aid' mentality that were really not present. *Gered Gereedschap* (Used Equipment) does not convey the spirit and commitment of the excellent Dutch Group. But *Tools for Solidarity*, Belfast, is straight to the point (and unlikely to cause such embarrassment as two TFSR staff members felt on being introduced to one ladies' coffee morning as being '... here to tell us all about *Tools for Self Relief*'). In practice, Newcastle Tool Aid, led by the cheerful Gary Jenkins, continued to cooperate with TFSR and relations were soon almost back to normal. Within the year, Gary was elected to the board of directors of TFSR. For a while we fretted over the constitutional problem of breakaway groups, but then the matter seemed to resolve itself, and we let it drop. GR

Growth and Consolidation
May 1986 – 1990

AFTER THIS UNHAPPY PERIOD, TFSR went from strength to strength. Put on their mettle by the AGM perhaps, directors decided to focus the first year of the Five Year Plan on much better support for the 50 local groups. David Crawford (Groups' organiser) made a survey of their needs and criticisms during the year, and found that most were small (5-6 members) and basically content with their level of representation within the TFSR membership structure. Annual costs were miniscule – on average about £60 a group! This was meagre, considering the thousands of pounds worth of value that groups generated each year. One key question was transport of kits to Netley Marsh and David and Pedro looked into this, trying to get special deals from road haulage companies. Up in Edinburgh, Paul Turner at the Garvald Centre tools group struck a particularly good deal with KSK freight, which brought their finished kits down to the south coast for years without charge.

The one disappointment that groups felt was in the lack of detailed feedback from village workshops overseas. 'We would like to know whether our solidarity is reciprocated,' wrote one refurbisher. Staff at Netley Marsh shared this feeling. Letters of thanks and blessing arrived quite often, with assurances that the tools would be of great value, but no details about the longer-term impact, or how artisans saw themselves in the wider social and political context. Some UK groups enclosed letters of greeting and photos with their tool kits, but had very limited response.

Refurbishing teams also wanted regular and better-produced copies of the quarterly newssheet *Elbow Grease* and other materials such as slide shows, videos and background papers on the countries and partners TFSR helped. 'Better produced' did not mean glossy, all good news and thanks from grateful recipients. Good-looking materials were fine, and it was great to report success, but most staff and directors wanted to use TFSR materials to stir things up a bit. If there were problems – about the quality of the tools sent, or snags in distribution, or on the wider questions of justice for the Third World – TFSR should make them known and take a clear stance. Some groups and members were dismayed at first, but even they found problems more interesting to read about than bland success stories. They

ABOVE Carpenters at Makanjiro Village, Tanzania, display furniture made using tools from TFSR (1986)

appreciated feeling part of a struggling organisation, and came up with their own views and practical suggestions. Sometimes *Elbow Grease* did receive negative comments from readers objecting to the 'partisan' content of its articles, and these were published in the hope of stimulating debate.

In London, Jan and Jackie Hoogendyk, Guy Davies and Robin Jenks were a driving force keen to set up a regional workshop and centre in the Camden area. Rents, of course, were frighteningly high, and the hunt for premises went on for many months, someone's garage being used for storing tools in the meantime. Finally, they found a unit on a mini-industrial estate in Kentish Town and the team set about building shelves, benches for refurbishing, an education area and a little office. Meanwhile, in the north, groups held a first meeting in Manchester and recommended that TFSR employ a regional fieldworker, for coordination, skills training (in refurbishing techniques) and development education.

Also in September, Gered Gereedschap (the Dutch tools organisation) and TFSR jointly sponsored the first Euro-tools Conference in Amsterdam. Thirty participants came from Denmark, Finland, France, Germany and the UK – the six Brits making an impressive entrance to the conference wearing black (cardboard) bowler hats. It was soon clear that the European groups were young and enthusiastic, but had given less thought than TFSR to development issues. They were satisfied to focus on tools, assuming that they would always do good. TFSR questioned this limited vision, and by the end of the conference the participants shared a broader insight into the complexities of development. Perhaps because of this, some proposed setting up a Pan European tools movement, but TFSR (fearing more bureaucracy) felt that each association should do things in its own way, while maintaining links with the rest.

In the autumn of 1986, the business consultants commissioned to make an appraisal of TFSR's operational system (as requested by the AGM) concluded: 'We feel that the vast resources channelled into the Netley Marsh site need time to show results. Results are now beginning to appear with the near completion of the [craft] work-shops, the exhibition and the [tools] workshop [...] all energies should be channelled into promoting and developing the local group structure, the Netley Marsh headquarters and the communication between them.' Although the firm had not provided adequate costings in this exercise, a difficult task, since everything would depend on what assumptions were built into those costings, TFSR members later met at an Extraordinary General Meeting in Manchester and effectively voted to retain the Netley Marsh site.

Paul Turner of the Garvald Tools group in Edinburgh reported another ground-breaking event in 1986. For some time they had been supplying refurbished equipment to the Glen Forest Training Centre in Harare, Zimbabwe, where

Shhhh! DON'T MENTION GLOBAL WARMING!

'I detect that you are falling into the trap, which has ensnared many overseas aid organisations, of engaging in domestic or global partisan politics. I refer particularly to your article on global warming and certain of your references to South Africa which appear to me to stray very far from your primary job of providing tools for Third World countries.'

LETTER, *ELBOW GREASE*, AUTUMN 1990

young blacksmiths upgraded their skills before returning to their villages. As a thank you, the Zimbabweans sent Paul a small selection of new tools made on their course. They were of excellent design and quality, and showed just what could be done. Directors became even more convinced that encouraging and supporting overseas tool production was a strategy that TFSR should follow.

Despite its unpromising start, 1986 saw a massive increase in the numbers of refurbished tools: 28,415 (40% to Nicaragua), bringing the running total to 81,061.

1987 Fundraising and fun – Covent Garden style

This year brought an end both to the European Community grant and to financial support from UNESCO, and TFSR suddenly had to focus on fundraising. Fortunately, most of the debt on Netley Marsh had been paid off, but running costs – for example for shipping, with the huge increase in tools output in 1986 – were growing fast.

Staff and directors looked at various fundraising schemes, and the pros and cons of employing a professional fundraiser. The main debate on fundraisers was whether to pay them a

> I'm interested in tools anyway, because anything basic – such as hand tools – is needed so much over there, and we're going beyond that now into a high-tech. situation. So many of these things are being thrown away, as we live in a waste economy, and that always offends me. So, for example, they have saws that you use for a couple of months, then throw away, and all that lovely material has gone – whereas people overseas would use them well and can't afford to buy them.
>
> [TFSR] seems to me a very good idea of sharing out what we have without interfering with other people's cultures and backgrounds. It helps them to help themselves, which is what you want. And being a socialist – the most important aspect of what I thought was socialism was its non-national or international nature – that is, that people the world over have the same basic needs, the same aspirations, however much it's masked by cultural differences. Basically, we all have the same needs – to eat, to feed our families and to live in peace. And this can help that a lot.
>
> **GUY DAVIES**, *TFSR LONDON*

ABOVE **The Garvald tools team. Paul Turner with saw, David Crawford, far right (1988)**

percentage of whatever they managed to bring in, which raised ethical questions, or pay them a regular salary however they fared, which would be a big gamble given the fragile state of the finances*.

The main individuals dealing with this were Mary Tolfree, who continued to do the increasingly complicated bookkeeping, taking special pride in producing lucid end of year accounts, and Kevin Petrie from Settle, Yorkshire. Kevin, no longer young, refurbished thousands of tools in his garage from 1979 until two months before his death in 2003. A vigorous Quaker and ex-company secretary, Kevin stuck at first to his refurbishing, but then joined the board of directors advising on finances. Sitting through so many meetings, he began to appreciate the wider issues about aid and development, which he found a real eye-opener. So much so that in 1987 he paid his way to Tanzania to learn more about living conditions there, the highlight of his trip being a long discussion with Mwalimu Julius Nyerere.

* One fundraiser, from REACH, a volunteer scheme for retired executives, was confident that he could raise £25,000 for TFSR in one year. 'Easy as falling off a log!' he burbled. A year later he said good-bye, having managed just £1,000, but – whether embarrassed by his early promises, or from a kind heart – he added a further £1,000 out of his own pocket.

GIANT SCREWDRIVER TURNS HEADS IN COVENT GARDEN

TFSR celebrated sending its 100,000th tool – a huge saw – in Covent Garden on 23rd September, in bright sunshine and before a large crowd. Four market stalls, giant polystyrene tools in psychedelic colours, an African jazz band, jugglers and buskers all had the crowd's attention. Lenny Henry and Richard Briers cavorted about, abetted by many TFSR supporters as the last countdown started – 99,990... 99,991... 99,992...'

The climax came at 4.30 when Richard and Lenny managed to sever a length of telephone pole using the razor-sharp two-man saw. This, the 100,000th tool, was part of a woodwork kit destined for the Young People's Development Organisation in Sierra Leone.

ELBOW GREASE, *AUTUMN, 1987*

Apart from UNESCO and the European Community, the major donors to date had mostly had a religious or ethical orientation, such as Christian Aid, the Joseph Rowntree Charitable Trust, the Peter Selwood Charitable Trust and several other very supportive trusts and charities. Frankly, they responded to the solidarity message far more readily than did trades unions or UK-based African groups, who it was first expected would become natural allies in a tools scheme to help fellow workers in Africa. Through the Charities Aid Foundation (CAF), Mary Tolfree spent time and effort setting up a Give as You Earn scheme, under which employees would donate a small percentage of their pay, deducted at source, to help TFSR. But though TFSR was chosen as a CAF Charity of the Year, Give as You Earn made only modest headway. More successful, a year or two later, was the Friends of TFSR scheme, which invited individuals to adopt the organisation, preferably by making a covenant and taking advantage of taxation laws that benefited registered charities.

For their part, local groups seemed to be raising funds successfully. The enterprising Crickhowell team, for example, with Tony Care, Harry and Ruth Iles and other lively members,

RIGHT Lenny Henry at Covent Garden (1987)

GROWTH AND CONSOLIDATION MAY 1986–1990

showed real flair with their Christmas bazaars, summer festivals, Bottle Tombolas and sales of whole foods, and managed to raise considerable sums to help the tools work along. And their tools work was impressive, with many kits brought to Netley Marsh in Tony's ancient Citroën.

At the Garvald group in Edinburgh, Paul's friend Phil Johnson helped run an Easter 'Forge-In' – a blacksmithing event where twenty-one smiths hammered out individual pieces of an elaborate wrought-iron gate for Edinburgh Zoo. This raised £500, shared between Netley Marsh workshops and a water pump appeal for Togo.

The biggest money-spinners, as mentioned, had been the *Week's Good Cause* appeals that had brought in £45,000 between them, but the BBC would not give an annual slot to a little-known organisation like TFSR. Somehow, the organisation needed a higher national profile. In the summer of 1987, a chance presented itself when records showed that TFSR had sent out over 98,500 tools. With 100,000 in sight, the opportunity seemed too good to miss...

TFSR also broke new ground that summer, with its new policy on the sale of tools. For years, it had followed the rule that once received on the doorstep tools could not be sold, yet some were obviously valuable, if too frail and ancient to be of any use in an African village. Over time, local groups had sent their antiques to Netley Marsh and they had filled up a storeroom. Dealers turned up too, with tempting offers – 'Give yer fifty quid for that old plane; I'm being generous' – but staff had no idea what to charge for antiques, and anyway were bound by the No Sales policy. Some of the most curious old tools went on display in the exhibition, but the rest simply gathered dust. Worse, they began to deteriorate.

The problem finally went to directors, who decided that such tools could now be sold centrally by a reputable auction house – thereby getting a fair market price – while any money raised should go into the Vice Fund. This fund covered the purchase of special tools, such as anvils and oil stones, which were always in short supply. Christie's of London held a tools action that summer, and boosted the Vice Fund with a cheque for nearly £2,000 – the 'fifty quid' plane having fetched over £600.

In the spring of 1987, TFSR invited Bishop Trevor Huddleston to become a patron of TFSR. He accepted, later suggesting that former-president Julius Nyerere of Tanzania might become a patron as well. This was an exciting prospect, but it also made matters more difficult. Julius Nyerere, also a world figure by any standards, must have had hundreds of major causes to lend his name to ahead of a small Northern NGO. But in another serendipity it turned out that Guy Davies of the London group had years previously rented a room in his house to a Miss Joan Wicken. And Miss Wicken was Personal Private Secretary to Julius Nyerere! It's not impossible that Joan and Trevor each put in a good word for TFSR. In any event, these two great men became joint-patrons – a considerable coup*.

That summer, Kevin joined Glyn to evaluate the use of TFSR tools in Tanzania, a study funded by the Nuffield Foundation. Accompanied by Mr. EZ Msuya, the first of several liaison officers appointed by SIDO to ensure continuous contact with TFSR, they visited fifty village workshops in six weeks, some of them very remote. The evaluation studied workshops in 1983, 1985 and 1987 to see how they were faring. This is not the place to detail all the findings. In brief, 27% had failed completely – tools stolen, no markets, lack of raw materials and conflict with the village authorities. 15% had started well, hit a bad patch in 1985 but recovered again by 1987 and 58% had functioned well over the whole period, their products and employment of benefit to the whole community.

On reaching Dodoma, designated capital of Tanzania, late one evening, they learned that Julius Nyerere had invited them to meet him the following afternoon. They piled into a bus, and rattled 300 miles through the night to reach Dar es Salaam next morning, hair and clothes matted with dust.

The session with Julius Nyerere was a revelation. They met him at his home on a palm-fringed shore of the Indian Ocean just north of Dar es Salaam. He fully understood the need of working people for basic tools. Indeed, he had long championed village blacksmiths, who were of low status in traditional society and had sometimes been banned under colonial rule. When they showed him a miniscule hand saw (exchanged for a new one with a carpenter) almost worn away by many years' sharpening, he exclaimed, 'Yes, but this man was lucky. *He had a saw.* The others *have no saw.*' He then talked about empowerment of people in rural areas, the need to find productive work for vast numbers of young unemployed Tanzanians, and how TFSR was doing something unique. He was so well

---

* Not that their names cut any ice with professional fundraisers. Rather the opposite. When we proudly named our two patrons at a London day course for fundraisers, eyebrows were raised. 'You'd do far better to get a Royal,' they urged, 'or someone big in the City.'

informed, humorous and positive that Kevin and Glyn left his house after a couple of hours walking on air*.

A day or two later, meeting with the Minister for Trade and Industry, they asked what he thought would best motivate village blacksmiths to make a wider range of tools and to improve their quality. The Minister suggested launching regional tool-making competitions. So before leaving Tanzania, together with SIDO, Glyn drafted guidelines for such competitions. TFSR would provide £300 in cash prizes, and all entrants would also receive equipment sent by TFSR, things they could not normally make themselves, such as anvils, files, drills and saws.

Over the next few years, over forty tool-making competitions were held around the country, and TFSR became ever more deeply involved in supporting tool production.

Rewarding though this visit to Tanzania was, they came back to Britain feeling dissatisfied. In a paper to a TFSR directors' meeting in August, Glyn wrote, '...alas, TFSR is not the radical 'development' organisation we'd like to think we are. Despite our literature + criteria, we fall far short in practice. On requests, our information is so scanty that we are really dishing out Aid packages to unknown recipients. Minimal exchange of ideas. We know almost nothing of the values that motivate their work. Likewise, the recipients know nothing of TFSR, what motivates us, our values. With the last 100,000 tools, valuable though they might have been, we have missed a great opportunity to exchange ideas and make it a people-to-people affair. So many one-off hand-outs to a wide range of applicants and many countries makes serious feedback impossible. Our Dev. Ed. is something of a butterfly, touching on various issues but not integrated into our overseas partners' work [...] another missed opportunity.'

In mid 1987, in view of this assessment and having sent tools to 28 different countries** since 1979, TFSR decided to concentrate on four Priority Countries – Tanzania, Zimbabwe, Mozambique and Nicaragua – and at a later meeting added Ghana and Sierra Leone, following a field trip there by Peter McDermott. This

---

* Well, not quite. After the bus ride from Dodoma, I had washed my dirty trousers at the YMCA thinking they would easily dry before our afternoon meeting. They didn't, and left a large dark stain in his leather armchair. I still feel guilty about it today! GR.

** Tanzania, Zimbabwe, Nicaragua, Uganda, Ghana, Sierra Leone, Gambia, Eritrea, Ethiopia, Kenya, Somalia, Botswana, Swaziland, Mozambique, Guinea Bissau, Zaire, Angola, Cameroon, Nigeria, Mauritius, India, Fiji, Bangladesh, Colombia, Dominica, St. Lucia, Grenada, Honduras.

gave a new focus and continuity, vital for building good working relationships with partner organisations, and also made shipping easier and less costly. However, it also meant having to turn down excellent requests from other countries, which was very hard, and the new policy was still breached in exceptional cases.

Bearing in mind Roger Rees's critique, directors now took on specialised roles and set up sub-committees: Employment, Finance, Netley Marsh and Groups, and Development Education. These gave each person the chance to develop an area of expertise and support a staff member. On the other hand, it required many more meetings and significantly more travel. Most, but not all, staff appreciated the development. For other areas such as partnership and requests, all directors continued to be equally involved.

A particular concern for the Netley Marsh sub-committee were Health and Safety, and Fire inspections of the workshop and other buildings. Confronted by mountains of sharp tools, ancient lifting gear, uneven lighting and insufficient fire exits... ashen-faced inspectors drew up lists of changes they required. Some of these would have cost a small fortune to carry out commercially, so staff and directors settled for 'home improvements' wherever possible, only spending serious money on key items such as specialised fire extinguishers. They then waited nervously for the officials' return visits. To everyone's relief, the inspectors proved very reasonable, grumbling a little here and there, but accepting that TFSR had tried to act responsibly, but lacked the financial resources of a profit-making company.

Meanwhile, several northern TFSR groups were still unhappy about the service they were getting from Netley Marsh, probably due to poor communication. They proposed setting up a northern forum, with a regional officer attached, and months went by with TFSR directors and northern groups trying to work out a system to fund this. It was complicated by the fact that some northern groups did not particularly want such a forum, fearing it might become a costly talking shop.

In late 1987, Robin Cluley moved on from Netley Marsh, having improved the workshops in many ways, especially by installing a dust-extraction system to protect volunteers on the grinders and rust brushes. Also in 1987, thanks to a relative of Eddie Grimble, the office acquired a strange new gadget: an Amstrad word processor. One afternoon, all the staff huddled round peering as its greenish screen lit up, some excited by its potential, others viewing it with deep suspicion.

> *TFSR tools have benefited 886 families from farming cooperatives, sewing cooperatives, carpentry workshops, training workshops and people in poor neighbourhoods. We think it is important to have contributed to the reconciliation process amongst those who were in different trenches (ex-army and ex-resistance). Now they use the tools in building, repair and horticulture, principally in Nueva Guinea and el Rama.*
>
> FACS, *NICARAGUA, 1992*

1988 - 1989 Visitors, major donors and a little blackmail

At Netley Marsh, Harry and Ruth Iles from Crickhowell TFSR replaced Robin, job-shared the workshop post and soon brought a family feel to the place. Harry was a natural teacher-philosopher and knew how to stimulate workshop volunteers' interest, connecting their efforts to the wider world. They would often down tools and gather round to debate some political or ethical point* – and then go back to refurbishing with great enthusiasm. Tools output certainly did not suffer.

In May, a particularly welcome visitor came, Mr EB Toroka, Director General of SIDO in Tanzania. Within an hour of his arrival, he was in overalls**, cleaning and sharpening tools for East Africa, but he spent most of his time talking with volunteers and staff about life in village communities and the promotion of small scale enterprises in Tanzania.

In London, at last, Jan Hoogendyk's dream came true and the Regional Workshop opened in Allcroft Road, Kentish Town, funded by local efforts and supported by a wonderful community of ANC activists in the Hampstead area who ran numerous open days and other public events. Jan and Robin Jenks became key people in the workshop, backed up by Mike Stevens, seconded from VSO for six months to involve local schools and community centres in development education. A while later they were joined by Andy Keen in the

---

* For example, some of the older men, kind-hearted and skilled as refurbishers, could nevertheless pass comments that were unwittingly very racist. Very diplomatically, Ruth and Harry did some re-educating, just 'chatting things over' in the whole group. By the end, everybody got the message, but with no hurt feelings.

** Most of our official visitors did some practical work. They enjoyed the novelty and it seemed to fix TFSR in their minds. In 1992, I was introduced to an African prime minister who had visited us years before in a lesser capacity. He shook hands and looked thoughtful. 'TFSR? Ah, yes. *You're* the people who had me lifting all those heavy boxes!' GR

Jan, exiled from apartheid South Africa and settled with his family in London, recruited me into his local group in 1985. He was an inspiring man. It wasn't just his work with tools, he was also very active in promoting the political dimension of TFSR's philosophy and this made a big impression on us. Jan was a great orator, he was amusing, lively, and always spoke from the heart.

Our group met weekly in a local community centre workshop. The downside of this was that Jan had to take the tools home afterwards in his little van. Their small flat was stacked with them – under the beds, in the kitchen – and his wife Jackie was very long-suffering. You can imagine the joy and relief on the domestic front when he found a permanent base for the group in Kentish Town, where the London Regional Centre opened in 1988.

His cheerful enthusiasm and skill soon gathered a large group of volunteers and the centre produced many valuable tool kits during its short life. Sadly, Jan's own health deteriorated markedly in 1989, and with it his practical input. I clearly remember a directors' meeting at the Centre on a cold, grey December morning, when a frail Jan Hoogendyk appeared at the door to say goodbye. He told us that his time with TFSR had been one of the most worthwhile periods of his life. It was a tearful moment.

The Centre closed a year later, after rent increases by Camden Council, but a local school – at which Jan had spoken several times – took up refurbishing work for TFSR.

TFSR AND JAN HOOGENDYK REMEMBERED **ROBIN JENKS**, TFSR LONDON

workshop and Kate Sebag running the regional programme for London and the Midlands.

1988 saw large consignments of tools go out to SIDO and the Nkowe Trade School in Tanzania, and to the Fundacion August César Sandino (FACS) and Building Brigades in Nicaragua – part of the Nicaragua Solidarity Campaign. As with support for the ANC, links to such programmes in Nicaragua gave a political dimension to TFSR's work, welcomed by staff and most, but not all, supporters. And news of TFSR's work must have reached President Daniel Ortega of Nicaragua, for on a visit to Edinburgh he remarked to Paul Turner, 'TFSR is an outstandingly positive

> *To pass on the tongs is to sustain and perpetuate the blacksmithery.*
>
> MWALIMU JULIUS NYERERE
> TRADITIONAL SAYING, IN HIS FAREWELL ADDRESS TO PARLIAMENT

action […] and there is so much more TFSR can do – building direct links with our artisans who need tools to work with'. Little could President Ortega know that a few months later Hurricane Joan would devastate the Atlantic coast of his country. On hearing of the destruction, TFSR prepared 77 mini-building kits, rushed them to Gatwick and an Oxfam plane that landed them in Managua next day. All done in 36 hours. A record.

On the regional front, negotiations between directors and local groups finally resulted in the ebullient David Crawford changing roles and opening a northern region office in Huddersfield. However, his first winter there was pretty lonely, seemingly out of touch with Southampton, yet struggling to generate practical cooperation between local groups.

Directors seemed to spend an unduly large part of 1988 on a tedious reappraisal of the *Articles & Memorandum of Association*. A Constitutional working party, heroically led by Dorothy Cussens, spent untold hours going through the document which, though in awful jargon, had served its purpose fairly well. After months of deliberation, correspondence, meetings, drafting sessions, debate with one especially pernickety member, and taking legal advice, the working party finally decided to leave things pretty much as they were. There is a lesson to be learned there, somewhere.

Meanwhile, the Netley Marsh site, with all buildings complete, looked smart and brought in annual rents of £11,000. TFSR's own offices, tools store, exhibition and house were rent-free – providing a huge sense of security. Workshop tenants came and left, but often provided a fascinating mix of craftsmen and women – a violin maker, a skilled German cabinet maker, a wrought iron specialist, a couple of young women sewing 'raunchy' (their term) underwear and swimsuits, garden machinery repairs, upholstery, fine pottery, a printer, stained glass, a caster of garden gnomes, and much else. However, the courtyards between the buildings were still a sorry mess, only partially surfaced and criss-crossed by muddy back-filled trenches. But this was to change, thanks to a little blackmail!

Following a visit to Netley Marsh, the Rev. Robin Ewbank of Bramshott, wrote to Peter McDermott in May 1988, 'I have probably dropped you right in it but I met the Princess Royal the day after my visit and mentioned TFSR…' A year later,

I would like to highlight a number of features of TFSR's approach which [my trustees] believe makes it rather different, and special, from other agencies working overseas.

Firstly, *TFSR has a real partnership model with the groups with whom it works abroad. At any one time there will be a number of overseas volunteers working at Netley Marsh, who will be informing and guiding policy. TFSR convenes regular conferences with its partners abroad, often raising money for their travel costs so they can attend. Earlier this year I attended a conference in Southampton and it was refreshing to hear representatives from Africa talk about their everyday problems. Frankly, not many NGOs are able to achieve this level of interchange, sharing and production of a joint agenda*

Secondly, *TFSR harnesses a huge number of volunteers here in the UK through a network of local groups, and also at Netley Marsh where volunteers have the opportunity to develop their skills and have job training.*

Thirdly, *TFSR maintains a critical and alert attitude to third world politics and issues. […]* **Fourthly**, *TFSR has remained a 'hands-on' organisation. It has sought to live within its means and its own self reliance. TFSR has avoided, again in contrast to other overseas projects, taking on programmes simply because there is funding available.*

TFSR ASSESSED **RODNEY HEDLEY**, THE HILDEN CHARITABLE FUND.

a red helicopter bearing Princess Anne landed on an adjacent field. She looked a little severe at first, confronted by a quotation from Tolstoy in large letters on the workshop wall: '**I SIT ON A MAN'S BACK, CHOKING HIM… ASSURING HIM THAT I WILL DO ALL I CAN TO HELP HIM – EXCEPT GET OFF HIS BACK**'. She then came face to face with Harry Iles's powerful sculpture, seven feet high, of two gnarled hands clasping each other: '**SOLIDARITY WITH NICARAGUA**'. The princess hesitated, then carried on resolutely, showed a growing interest and began to ask some searching questions. At tea, she made several critical yet informed comments about Tanzania's policies. Staff, notably Harry, Ruth and Mary, did not defer to her opinions but put up a lively defence. To her credit, Princess Anne in turn came back with vigorous counter-arguments, and postponed her departure flight by 20 minutes to let the debate continue.

> *We were in business. We'd been in business for ten years and at that time our son who was on holiday in Yugoslavia was killed in a road accident. It was then we really started to think about our lives, and we thought that life wasn't all about making money. So we changed and we've been doing charity work more or less ever since. Before, we were inward-looking – our family was the only thing that mattered. And now we're outward-looking and everyone's our family.*
>
> DEREK TAYLOR *DONCASTER TFSR*

When she had left, staff and helpers scoffed the remaining cream cakes and looked out over the beautifully asphalted courtyards – all laid free by Hampshire County Council. 'You don't want a Royal ankle to be sprained in *Hampshire*, do you?' Glyn had asked them a few weeks earlier. And, no, apparently they didn't.

'TFSR's plan to promote tool-making overseas took a big step forward in 1988-9 when the CEC (Commission of European Communities) granted £150,000 for a three-year programme with SIDO (Tanzania). The project was to support 14 blacksmithing/tool-making units and budgeting for this had fully occupied Mary for some months. Blacksmithing kits, tool designs and scrap steel were prepared for Tanzania and Ian Backhouse, then Chairman of TFSR, made a four-week visit of the units to clarify their needs and potential.

In the UK, the northern region saw a marked increase in activity following David Crawford's move. He visited all local groups several times, encouraged the formation of eight new groups and ran a Training Weekend for them at Bakewell in Derbyshire, along with the local TFSR, with entertaining instruction in saw sharpening given by Harry Lawton. The London Region Centre was also getting into gear, producing increasing numbers of tools and kits, running fundraising events and organising training days.

With these new developments and the arrival of Ruth Heine as Groups/Overseas Secretary, staff numbers in TFSR increased to eight. Wanting to capture the vitality and variety of our refurbishing teams, from the South coast to Edinburgh, Ruth, Andy Keen and Glyn visited ten of them to film a video, *'Keeping Something Alive'*.

But extra staff meant growing costs and the financial year for 1988-9 saw expenditure rise to £107,471 – a level no one could have dreamt of ten years earlier. TFSR received grants from the European Commission, the Joseph Rowntree Charitable Trust, Young Friends (Quakers), the States of Guernsey Overseas Aid Committee, the Hilden Charitable Fund, the Leigh Trust, Christian Aid, Hampshire County Council, the AB and MC Gillett Charitable Foundation, the Nuffield Foundation and – Daisy and Harold Backhouse, who for many years made and sold fine crafts to raise funds. These individuals and charitable trusts, and many more besides, supported TFSR year in, year out, making a really valuable contribution to the work. It was not always easy to find the right words to thank them, but perhaps they, too, realised the multiplier-effect that their cash produced in terms of value at home and overseas.

This was the period, too, when TFSR started to improve staff conditions. Already in 1986, proper contracts of employment had been drawn up and staff began to receive salaries. At first these were modest, in the region of £4,000 a year, with annual reviews based on changes in the Retail Price Index. Later discussions concerned the relative merits of equal pay versus pay that would provide incentives and recognise special responsibilities. At a meeting in September 1989, directors stated that, 'TFSR aims to have an equal pay policy, although exceptions will be made for the post of Coordinator and in the payment of a single increment to staff who remain longer than two years'. Staff responded by welcoming the equal pay policy (by now £6,300 p.a.) but turned down the idea of increments, feeling that this would undermine team spirit. Within a year or so, TFSR also planned to become an Equal Opportunities employer, but concluded that a pension scheme for staff was still beyond its means.

1990 *News from the groups and the regions*

This was the year when the SIDO/TFSR tool-making and blacksmithing programme in Tanzania really took off. Mary Tolfree worked late hours to acquire an Isuzu truck from Japan and get it shipped to Dar es Salaam. Once there, it became the work-horse of the programme, taking loads of tools and scrap steel over terrible roads and dirt

YOU REALLY CAN'T COMPLANE...

From the Sheffield group, TFSR learned that Stanley Tools Ltd. sold off its reject plane blades to a scrap dealer at a derisory price. Netley Marsh offered to buy them, so as to send out each refurbished plane with 6 new blades, and so prolong its useful life. Stanley agreed and even offered to deliver them, but on one condition: TFSR must accept all the blades each month. Once started, the supply could not be turned off and on. And so the sharp, shiny blades began to arrive, hundreds of them, thousands of them – wonderful!

After a year there must have been 50,000 filling the back store. Boxes bursting at the seams. Staff dreaded the arrival of each new truck-load from Sheffield. Finally, TFSR had to admit defeat and cancelled the scheme, never having imagined that the industrial process could generate so much waste.

LEFT A sewing machine training day. TFSR Doncaster (1986)

tracks to remote blacksmithing units. SIDO organised four Regional toolmaking competitions nationwide and a three-week skills-exchange for smiths in Tabora. TFSR also helped the Tanzanian Folk Development Colleges' tool-making programme, providing tools and steel to fifteen units, with funding from the Nuffield Foundation and the UNESCO Co-Action scheme.

By this time, TFSR's northern and southern regions were getting into their stride. David Crawford married a Finnish TFSR volunteer and left for Helsinki, so Harry and Ruth moved to Sheffield to service 19 local groups, including Glasgow, Belfast and Chester. Doncaster was particularly lively and ran one of the first sewing machine training days with 40 people from nine groups learning the intricacies of a Singer's works and turning out 20 reconditioned machines by the end of the day. Since then, TFSR groups have held scores of such training days and weekends.

In the south, the number of TFSR groups increased to 18, one of the most noteworthy being in Milton Keynes at the Camphill Community, where five people with special needs and two co-workers (John Halliwell and Bill Jones) turned out seven beautiful kits in their first year. The London centre was used to full capacity, with refurbishing, an international voluntary workcamp and several meetings of TFSR directors. One of these meetings was particularly sad, though, as Jan Hoogendyk joined us to say farewell. His cancer was clearly advanced and he died that summer. In June, a further blow fell: the London Regional Centre had to close because of a hefty rent-rise by Camden Council, but Kate carried on her regional work supporting groups such as Sally Newcombe's in Westminster.

The south west and Wales region was also active, with nine groups, from Plymouth to Holt to Cardiff, each with its own quirky character. The Isle of Wight TFSR, for example – held together by John and Judith Fulford – had the most romantic freight system of anywhere in the UK. They filled their sailing boat to the gunnels* with refurbished equipment every six months and sailed across the Solent from Cowes to the old smugglers' village of Buckler's Hard. Waiting on the quayside (in the dark o' the moon, with the Excise men safe in the King's Head) would be TFSR's ancient van, ready to load the booty and slip away through the New Forest to Netley Marsh.

---

* Loaded almost literally to the gunnels on one occasion, but putting off crossing the Solent because of bad weather, they returned to the mooring next day to find just their mast showing above water!

> What attracts me to TFSR is that it encompasses a bit of everything: it's recycling, it's helping people who need tools in other countries, it's using people's skills in this country... To me, it's the ideal Green development organisation.
>
> TONY CARE, *TFSR CYMRU*

The Crickhowell team was one of the most remarkable TFSR groups in the whole of Britain. They had more great characters involved than it's possible to name, but Tony Care was the driving force. Quite apart from their regular collecting and refurbishing, the Crickhowell folk were brilliant at organising events and getting the TFSR message across to the public. One such initiative was their blacksmithing stall at a particularly muddy Glastonbury Festival with the participation of Enock Ndondole from SIDO, using genuine African goatskin bellows to heat the charcoal fire. The ringing anvil, gaudy banners and photo display drew the crowds and generated plenty of discussion. Crickhowell became masters in running such outdoor events over the years, amongst them – Glastonbury, the Big Green Gathering, Cwmdu camps and Green & Away. Everywhere, old and young would gather round asking questions, wanting to work at the anvil or refurbish tools. As the campfire burned low at the end of a long hard day, weary volunteers would crawl into their tents, leaving Tony still chatting away with a friend or two. But first thing next morning he would be up and about, fire rekindled and a big kettle of tea already brewed*.

The year saw 50,000 refurbished tools shipped overseas, but also a renewed debate as to whether TFSR was principally concerned with solidarity or technical assistance. The Overseas Development Administration (ODA – British Aid programme) was keen to promote small scale enterprise overseas and had grants available for organisations like TFSR, if it chose to go down this route. On the one hand, TFSR was already supporting thousands of small businesses, cooperatives, women's groups and the like, in carpentry, tailoring, building, motor mechanics, tool-making and much more. But against this, was it ready to become a cog in an official Aid machine, especially one run by a government that was cutting its

---

* The Crickhowell team went on to pioneer much else under the name of *TFSR Cymru*, setting up a first-class workshop of their own, and developing especially close contacts with blacksmith communities in Mwanza Region, Tanzania.

Aid budget and shifting the onus onto the 'wonderful work done by voluntary organisations'? This was one of the matters discussed at the bracing 1989 Annual Conference in Blackpool.

The Annual Conference – a weekend event – was an occasion when one and all in TFSR (and in particular, any visitors from partner organisations in Africa) could get together, report back on their year's work, and raise any questions. Staff, volunteers and visitors met in simple accommodation such as a community centre, church hall or school. Mattresses or sleeping mats were often supplied or participants brought their own sleeping bags and signed up on arrival for the cooking rota, washing up, crèche supervision, etc. The Friday evening was always a relaxed affair, perhaps slide shows of recent field trips to Africa, with hot soup and rolls kept available for anyone arriving late.

The 1990 Annual Conference was held at a high school near Hebden Bridge in Yorkshire. The assembly hall housed discussions, entertainment and displays, with the classrooms used as sleeping quarters. Saturday morning saw some good discussions about North-South partnership in response to a paper from ORAP, Zimbabwe. Central

...I found myself at the Garvald Centre with Paul Turner and a group of young people with special needs. Paul took me under his wing in a totally unsexist, unpatronising and supportive way, ready to share his vast knowledge. This is something many men prefer to keep under wraps. They confuse and discourage us with complicated and unnecessary language.

Later, I set up a TFSR group as part of a work project for people with mental health difficulties in Westminster. This runs every Wednesday with ten of us (two women, one more soon to be recruited). It's the most popular of the work projects and brings a sense of pride and value not only to the group but also to the centre as a whole. The members love it! My manager loves it! His manager loves it! And, most important, we know how vital the tools are to our friends overseas.

SALLY NEWCOMBE, *WESTMINSTER*

> *Christian worship asks more of you than just coming to Church once a week. It cries out for actual action. I find that TFSR is the outlet for me.*
>
> MELVYN FIELDING,
> BLACKPOOL TFSR

to ORAP's analysis was power and the power relationships that lie at the heart of underdevelopment, both in the industrialised world and in Zimbabwe. They questioned TFSR's claim to empower working people overseas, and asked: '*The Western public who support ORAP – have they the power, either to change their own situation or the international forces which impact on us? What does empowerment mean for donors and recipients?*'

Harry Iles and Mark Smith led some far-reaching discussions in working groups and at a plenary session, and TFSR later sent its conclusions to ORAP, hoping to develop a deeper dialogue. Participants at the Hebden Bridge conference felt that they were really thinking things through at last. (Unfortunately ORAP did not keep up the correspondence, possibly due to the huge political pressures upon them in southern Zimbabwe at that time and more critically in recent years.)

After lunch, more discussions, and then a two-hour walk along beautiful Calderdale, followed by supper and an evening practising circus skills, taught by a professional group. Then music, a bar (with casks of beer furnished by Crickhowell, as always) and general socialising.

They spent Sunday morning looking at the UK scene and hearing reports from local TFSR groups. This gave everyone a chance to recount their successes or raise problems – local and regional, with Netley Marsh or with TFSR as a whole. (Usually, no formal decisions were made, but directors and staff took note and some matters went on to the agenda for a directors' meeting.) Then lunch, tidy up and depart. The formula for this Annual Conference was followed pretty closely every year.

In June, 1990, TFSR hosted the 3rd International Workshop of Tools-Sending Organisations at Netley Marsh (essentially the original 'Euro-tools' group, but now with participants from Africa too). This had some 40 participants and included observers from UNESCO and the Overseas Development Administration (ODA). It was in some ways a prelude to a whole new stage in the development of TFSR, as it set out to influence the thinking and policies of large professional agencies.

Finally, on a personal note, Mark and Sheila Smith had returned to Gosport

ABOVE **Harry Iles introduces ORAP's philosophy at the Hebden Bridge Annual Conference (1990)**

from Zimbabwe earlier in the year and in September, Mark joined TFSR as Coordinator (Operations). As such, he was to oversee all the practical side of the programme, plus staff matters and the running of Netley Marsh. At the same time, after eleven busy years and glad to shed some responsibilities, Glyn became Coordinator (Resources & Development) – a fancy title for planning and fundraising.

Towards the New Millennium

1991–1995

THE EARLY NINETIES SAW TFSR opening up in various ways, perhaps spurred on by ORAP's challenge to demonstrate commitment to genuine partnership by actively setting out to influence powerful organisations on the world scene: the United Nations*, the European Community and the UK's official Aid programme. TFSR's message would certainly concern tools, but tools in the context of such issues as waste in consumer societies, pollution and destruction of the environment, refugees, the role of minorities, race and gender, Third World debt, unemployed young people and the urgent need for sustainable modes of development. Quite an agenda!

To achieve this, it was important to clarify TFSR's own values. Discussions with local groups resulted in the document 'Shared Values', but it was also informed by overseas partner organisations, learning from them, and discovering how far their principles matched TFSR's. Directors wanted them, increasingly, to define the needs, express the problems and set the agenda for action. TFSR planned a programme of exchanges, for face-to-face contact and dialogue, inviting African partners to meet TFSR groups in the UK, and encouraging (a limited number of) TFSR activists to visit partners' programmes in Africa. Directors also decided that TFSR would organise conferences, both in Britain and Africa, bringing together partners to see what common ground existed and work out joint strategies that everyone (hopefully) could approve.

All of this was to take a lot of organising, and considerable sums of money. And all these plans were on top of the regular refurbishing work, plus the new blacksmithing/tools-production schemes in East Africa. Staff and directors were ready for the challenge**.

With a new Millennium on the horizon, the United Nations was preparing a global conference in Rio on Environment and Development – two subjects close to the heart of TFSR – so Glyn went to

---

* One campaign was to persuade the UK to rejoin UNESCO. Mrs Thatcher had withdrawn the United Kingdom from this UN agency in 1984 (along with the USA and Singapore), and for an astonishing 12 years Britain sat out in the cold.

** At Netley Marsh there were Tim Blumfield (Workshop organiser) assisted by Lawrence Foday, Ruth Heine (Overseas Secretary), Peter McDermott (Development Education worker), Mary Tolfree (Finance Officer), Mark and Glyn. Plus Neil Corney (Northern worker), Debra Dilcock (London/Midlands worker). The directors at that time were: Robina Jordan (Chair), Tony Care, Dorothy Cussens, Judy Connor, Robin Jenks, Arthur Marsh and Harry Iles. Gill Downey was Financial Adviser and Eddie Grimble Hon. Secretary.

lobby a major UN preparatory conference in Geneva in August. He soon realised, though, that while delegates from Africa fully agreed with the TFSR message in private, nobody was prepared to speak up for simple technology at an official level. Sharp suited diplomats lounged in the bars, thick documents by the thousand were photocopied on to non-recycled paper, and the lights at the UN *Palais des Nations* blazed away day and night. It was all very disheartening.

In the less privileged world, the SIDO/TFSR tools production project had got off to a good start. Muhintiri village was one of the 14 units in Tanzania, producing tools and training unemployed youth. In 1990, Muhintiri's Party Secretary, S.S. Chaurembo had voiced the anxiety of villagers and government officials when he said, 'I am most concerned about youth unemployment, young people just hanging about – they may drink, get into trouble. This Blacksmith's Group can help solve the problem.' A year later, the blacksmithing unit with seven apprentices had also spawned a rural services centre accommodating carpenters, tailors and cobblers, giving training to more unemployed youth. Marko Deu, the most highly skilled smith at Muhintiri, wrote to TFSR in 1991, 'Muhintiri's work has been much praised, especially for the agricultural implements, household items and clothes it now produces.'

All told, smiths in the SIDO-EC-TFSR project made over 20,000 tools in their first year and 30,000 more the following season. It was to be a good year for refurbishing too, with 51,000 tools sent out from Netley Marsh, including 755 sewing machines.

These record numbers of refurbished tools meant that, by Saturday 26th October 1991, it was time to celebrate again – the despatch of TFSR's quarter millionth tool, an event geared to coincide with the Annual Conference at the Friends Meeting House in Sheffield.

Stalls, banners, entertainment, music and giant polystyrene tools attracted passers-by to a brightly decorated shipping container near Sheffield town hall, as piles of tools were passed through the crowds to be loaded into it. In the afternoon, following a Global Any Questions in the Mandela Room of the town hall, TFSR launched *'VISION 2000'* – one aim of which was a million tools (sent and locally produced) by the end of the century. Then the 250,000th tool, a shining anvil, was presented to the Tanzanian Trade Counsellor, Mr Simon Mlay, and the evening was given over to Abasindi Traditional African Dance, the Sheffield Red Choir, a musical comedy *'That's What Tools Are For'* from Gosport, Small World's brassy dance music and more, late into the night.

Those who woke early enough next morning heard Bishop Trevor Huddleston give his second BBC *Week's Good Cause* appeal. It produced another amazing response, bringing in over £40,000. One scruffy envelope, with no covering letter, contained £80 in notes.

In every respect, 1991 was a happy year and a cheerful TFSR poster by Annie and Ken Meharg, with rainbow colours and a striking design (see title page) caught the mood nicely.

1992 Making known the good news – and the bad

The spring edition of *Elbow Grease* contained an article entitled 'Does the Blacksmith Have a Future in Africa?' The author, David Harries explained just why the smith is so vital as a maker and mender of equipment in the community. Some time later, David came to play an important role in TFSR, spending ten years on the board of directors (renamed Trustees).

A spring Annual General Meeting in Oxford approved *Shared Values* as the organisation's basic statement of principle. Its key headings were: *One world/Preventing waste/Small is effective/Partnership & solidarity/Self Reliance/and Building self-confidence.* Those at the AGM were particularly pleased that Tanzanian members of TFSR had put up their own motion asking the organisation to 'lobby the rich countries to set aside development funds for alleviating the lack of tools in the poorest countries', a clear message from African partners. Peter Rooke of the Oxford group, Harry Iles and Charles Hirom joined the board of directors, with Charles taking a special responsibility for finances. Dorothy Cussens became Chairperson, and Uganda was selected as a new priority country.

But there was tough debate too. Glyn and Mark were criticised by several groups for launching a *Tools for Change* campaign, cooperating with DIY giant B&Q. This followed a meeting with Alan Knight, B&Q's environmental adviser, appointed to change its previously questionable environmental policies. The two coordinators put the counter-argument, that B&Q was now committed environmentally, and that a joint campaign would reach a wider public. (What to make of the B&Q Leicester store manager, for example, who – disappointed at the few tools donated to TFSR by customers, – plastered the collection cage with publicity and personally towed it around town by tractor to generate local interest?) The *Tools for Change* campaign continued, but the AGM instructed TFSR to press B&Q to replace tropical hardwoods with sustainable timber within three years*.

---

* Soon after, B&Q decided to buy its tropical woods from sustainable sources, via the Forest Stewardship Council (FSC). The decision was probably made with scant regard to TFSR – but who knows?

In response to the Tanzanian motion at the AGM, TFSR organised a tools seminar for African diplomats at the Tanzanian High Commission in London, where Glyn and Mark urged them to recognise the potential of simple technologies, and to include these when they were drawing up Aid projects with wealthy donors. This followed advice received from Sir Sonny Ramphal at the Commonwealth Secretariat in the spring of 1992. 'Encourage the voice of Africa to be heard', he said, with particular reference to the problem of youth unemployment facing most Third World countries.

Research and Evaluation

Members, staff and directors were also aware of the constant need for research and evaluation of their work with partners overseas. This was emphasised in dealings with Comic Relief whom TFSR had approached for funds. Initially rather sceptical about its development credentials because of the jaunty TV programmes, TFSR staff found the Comic Relief team extremely well informed, putting the most searching questions – not least about evaluation.

TFSR measured its success in different ways. The number of tools shipped per year was an obvious indicator, but was by no means the best. More important was to ask:

- how many kits have arrived and been put to use by how many artisans?

- how far have increases occurred in production, sales, employment and income?

- how many communities have benefited – and in what ways?

- to what extent are new initiatives partner-led?

In Lindi Region, Tanzania, Mr Kh. Mapondela, ex-Principal of Nkowe and a member of TFSR, carried out a six-month study of tools issued to Nkowe trainees. His major finding was that, while 99% of kits did reach the villages, only 60% of the trainees returned home and few of them formed cooperative groups to make use of the tool kits. This was a real disappointment to all concerned, in view of the years of collaboration with the trade school and the thousands of tools sent to Lindi Region. Mr Mapondela's evaluation caused a major rethink at every level.

One aspect of the problem concerned ownership of the tools already sent. On returning to their villages, young Nkowe graduates rarely established new working groups due to their lack of status within the community. Village leaders did not feel confident about reallocating the unused tool kits to other artisans. TFSR directors recommended that SIDO, Lindi, negotiate the redistribution of the large kits, often held by the trainees' own family, to other artisans in the village community. Recognising that this broke with one of TFSR's early criteria (that tools should go to groups, not individuals) they also agreed with reluctance that future Nkowe graduates should receive personal mini-kits, even though many would probably seek work outside their home areas.

A second issue was the circulation of these findings to TFSR groups and grant-making trusts in Britain. Although the report would cause consternation, and might undermine morale, directors decided to be frank about the failure, not least because they had found that in the past bad news seldom resulted in a loss of support. So long as TFSR tackled its problems in a responsible way, members and funders showed not only patience, but responded with new interest, concern and support.

Later in the year, Harry Iles and Tim Blumfield travelled around Sierra Leone with partner organisations, the Association for Rural Development and the Council of Churches of Sierra Leone to evaluate the programme there. Here too, they concluded, TFSR should respond more to the actual needs of each working community, rather than providing standard kits of tools.

In Tanzania, Mark Smith and Enock Ndondole of SIDO made a detailed assessment of year III of the blacksmithing/tool production programme. Things had gone really well, though rural smiths were desperate for more scrap steel which, frustratingly, was still being bought up by dealers and exported to India.

On 9th July, Oliver Tambo of the African National Congress handed over the Solomon Mahlangu Freedom College to President Mwinyi of Tanzania and a short time later, TFSR received a letter from the ANC saying, 'It is our hope that [the college] will remain as a lasting symbol of the generosity of the host country and of the many donors and support groups, including TFSR.'

By the end of 1992, a record 43 tonnes of scrap steel and 53,346 refurbished tools, including 694 sewing machines had been sent out, bringing the cumulative tools total to 310,789. One thing did cause directors regret, though: they had to turn down 181 requests, from a wide range of countries, confirming what they already knew, that TFSR alone could never meet the need for tools in even one of its priority countries. As the Tanzanians had said, a major task remained: how to get governments and larger development agencies to recognise the importance of the artisan and agricultural sectors.

Many different concerns were therefore on the agenda at the Conference on Youth Unemployment, Partnership and the Importance of Tools for Development, 9-13th November, in Arusha,

QUOTES FROM THE CONFERENCE

Our rural craftsmen and women don't have basic tools. That's why our contact with TFSR is so important... Our governments talk about development, but when they go for loans, they think about big projects, they forget the needs of our people.

FRANCIS ATTA DONKOR, *VOLUNTARY WORKCAMPS ASSOCIATION OF GHANA*

I cannot emphasise strongly enough the critical need for tools that exists in Uganda as we embark on reconstruction.

GRACE AKELLO, *PRESIDENTIAL COMMISSION FOR TESO, UGANDA*

within sight of Mount Kilimanjaro. Organised jointly by SIDO and TFSR, it brought together 42 participants from ten countries, the Tanzanian Prime Minister, Julius Nyerere and Bishop Trevor Huddleston. Participants assessed their work over the past twelve years, considered the potential and problems of tool-making, including the export of scrap steel, and drew up an action plan. This laid out the principles and practicalities of cooperation for the years 1993-96.

The conference also produced a Charter: 'Youth and Tools for Sustainable Development', which began: *Youth unemployment is a social and economic time bomb. It demeans each affected person, wasting lives and talents. It threatens the future of every society, particularly in Africa. Nobody seems to have an answer to the problem – yet an answer is demanded by hundreds of millions of young people.*

We [...] believe there is an answer: The artisan sector of society, which has existed since time immemorial producing goods and services, is today ignored and starved of resources. It is virtually excluded from national development plans. Yet it has great potential for turning the ideal of 'popular participation' into daily reality. It opens up job opportunities to the majority of men and women in the population...

And, not surprisingly, it urged those in power – North and South – to think of tools when drawing up Aid requests, and to question the value of technologies that are not sustainable.

The conference had a really positive atmosphere. Eating, drinking, talking, singing and dancing was a wonderful experience and everyone got to know each other in those five days. People who before had been simply work contacts, or signatures at the bottom of a letter, became friends, and many of those friendships have lasted ever since. Tanzania banned the export of scrap steel several months later – perhaps the conference influenced government thinking in some way.

Back at Netley Marsh, another excellent long-term volunteer had arrived, Florian Köhler, doing non-military service. In Edinburgh, the Garvald group had refurbished their 100th kit of tools; Chester their 50th. Countrywide, TFSR was responding to another disaster in Nicaragua – a tsunami, which in a matter of minutes had destroyed the homes of over 10,000 people. Nicaragua's struggle against the forces of nature and US-backed Contra guerrillas was brought home vividly to refurbishing teams in the north by Sonia Cano of a Nicaraguan NGO, FACS, who described how refurbished tools were helping her people to survive and to improve their living conditions.

Manchester TFSR ran a 'Women and Wood' course as part of International Women's Week, where two City and Guilds women carpenters worked with

> *Great to find out that most of these things are ridiculously simple – just a matter of having the right tools and someone non-condemning to watch you to begin with.*
>
> 'FIVER' AFTER A WOMEN'S WEEKEND

14 female participants, learning about tools and then using them to make wooden crates. This course was similar to those run by-women-for-women, at Netley Marsh and elsewhere ever since Mary Atkinson had raised the issue in 1983. Basically, as Mary pointed out, women and girls are seldom encouraged to try their hand with tools, and so lack confidence. But after a weekend sharpening chisels on the grinder, drilling wood out of a broken hammer head or bashing lumps of red hot steel on the anvil, and generally discussing the whole issue, women gain the confidence to tackle heavier technical tasks. And why shouldn't they? In Africa, women use tools all the time in agriculture and, more recently, in carpentry, metalwork and motor mechanics.

By now, TFSR had over 100 regular collecting points around the country and 65 refurbishing groups, from well established ones like Belfast, running workcamps for Nicaragua and Namibia,

ABOVE **Women's weekend. London Region TFSR (1992)**

to a brand-new team set up in Coventry involving a skilled old craftsman, Arthur Astrop, and one of TFSR's most loyal supporters, Freda Rees*.

In 1992, too, Peter McDermott left TFSR after making a great contribution since 1984 developing educational materials and being a friendly and steadying presence during some difficult times. From then on, TFSR's development education activities were de-centralised to the regions.

One bonus for 1992 came as a result of Mary Tolfree's initiative and tenacity. For years, TFSR had paid VAT on all the new tools bought from the Vice Fund – anvils, files and many other pieces of special equipment – to include in kits. Despite having been told that the VAT could not be reclaimed, Mary began to dig into the legislation and to lobby contacts in Parliament. Finally, Customs & Excise gave way and Mary spent long evenings going through all the records and receipts for the previous nine years, work which produced a nice little refund of £18,000.

---

* Freda cheerfully conceded that she knew little about tools, but she was happy to organise, publicise, and seek out useful contacts – which was not really the forte of 'her gentlemen' who rather preferred refurbishing.

1993 What's yours – cheese & pickle or chips & mayonnaise?

In January, Mr EB Toroka, Director General of SIDO, reported that his organisation had distributed 180,000 tools from TFSR to more than 2,400 small enterprises throughout Tanzania, including carpenters, tailors, blacksmiths, masons, cobblers and motor mechanics.

Also in the New Year, fired by enthusiasm from the Arusha Conference, staff set about contacting allies who might help take TFSR's tools message to the world. An early, and most unlikely, advocate was local MP Michael Colvin, pro-fox hunting, pro-shooting, gentleman farmer Conservative, with strong White South African links. Amazingly, he supported TFSR right away, whatever his opinion of its anti-apartheid stance. Perhaps this sympathy arose from his very first meeting at Netley Marsh when he and his wife came for lunch - a simple affair: basically bread and cheese, pickle, salad and biscuits. As guests neared the house, Glyn slipped ahead to check that all was well. It wasn't: the resident cat crouched on the table, sampling the Cheddar. In a flash, cat was slung out, cheese squared off and parings tossed into the wood-burning stove – just as guests entered the room. Did Colvin feel some deep compassion for TFSR at that meal, seeing what tiny portions of protein everybody got?

With his support, TFSR gave a two-hour reception and presentation in the House of Commons on the 8th March, and it was good to see Frank Judd among several other well-known MPs (of all parties) who came to the event. The very next day, Mark, Mary, Dorothy Cussens and Glyn were in Brussels at the European Community, running a seminar for officials and representatives concerned with the EC's development programme. Back in Britain, scores of TFSR members wrote to their MPs and to Baroness Lynda Chalker (Minister for Overseas Development). As a result, 109 MPs signed an Early Day Motion supporting their approach. TFSR met with the Overseas Development Administration immediately afterwards, to discuss tool production in Sierra Leone and Ghana, which Tony Care and Neil Corney had visited to meet potential partners. Later, it was back to the House of Commons to set up a week-long exhibition in one of the lobbies. Heady with optimism, the team even cut a 'demo disc', 'Tools for Africa'. It never exactly topped the charts, but did get an airing on the BBC World Service.

In March, invited to a UN conference in Tokyo, Glyn took the chance to meet up with Julie and Monte Cassim (Eddie Grimble's sister and brother-in-law) in Nagoya to help set up an arm of TFSR in Japan. This association, based at a saw mill way up in the forests, later sent

> *This house notes that Tools for Self Reliance is launching the Arusha Charter on Youth & Tools for Sustainable Development on the 8th March 1993; recognises the enormous challenge posed by youth unemployment in the developing world; acknowledges the potential of tools, imported and locally produced, to provide jobs for the young and involve them in self-reliant development; believes that simple hand tools are a cost-effective, appropriate, environmentally friendly technology without which developing countries cannot develop; calls upon relevant Government Departments and major aid agencies to recognise that tools are an important element in overseas development aid and to consider the allocation of greater resources to tool provision and local tool production in Africa.'*
>
> **EARLY DAY MOTION** *TOOLS FOR CHANGE: A NEW COST-EFFECTIVE STRATEGY FOR AID TO THE THIRD WORLD*

equipment mostly to Sri Lanka. Now TFSR had sister groups in Australia, Austria, Denmark, Finland, France, Germany, Ireland, Japan and the Netherlands.

In May, a descent into the Underworld. Some time before, a friend of TFSR had found himself (as one does) at a dinner given by the Lord Mayor of London. Seated beside an industrial baron from Bolton, he had mentioned TFSR, and the Lancastrian had wondered if his firm could help, not in cash, but in kind. What did they make? The steel wheels for locomotives and rolling stock. Could they cast anvils? Of course! So it was that Glyn, Neil and an elderly Ruth Roberts reached Bolton one afternoon and entered a dark edifice straight out of Dante's *Inferno*. The heat and noise were intense. Furnaces blazed incandescent in the gloom, machines screeched in agony, slicing through solid metal, and men in goggles tramped about in the thick black dust, seemingly unconcerned as molten steel spilled and splashed around them – and into 24 superb anvil-shaped moulds, each one lettered: *TOOLS FOR SELF RELIANCE*.

Back on Earth, TFSR's network continued to expand, with 67 refurbishing teams and a further 115 groups collecting regularly on its behalf. Many attended the Annual Conference, with its theme *Questioning Development*, hosted by Chester TFSR. Sheffield TFSR ran a workcamp with Harry Lawton showing volunteers from India and Morocco how to sharpen saws. The Leicester group

ABOVE **A long way from Bolton. Specially cast TFSR anvils (1993)**

impressed locals with a tool-making weekend using an African forge, and Milton Keynes Camphill community celebrated their 50th kit with song, dance and Latin American food during Central America Week. Each team had something distinctive – Exeter was housed in a huge old mill overlooking the river; Sway occupied a stable; Manchester moved out of a cold, damp cellar into a dry, light one; Garvald sang the praises of its new sandblasting equipment (wonderful for zapping the rust off uneven surfaces); Gosport recommended carol singing as a fund raising method; and Crickhowell stuck by its well-tried formula of community fairs, summer camps and chips & mayonnaise for the helpers every Thursday evening.

From the early days TFSR welcomed people with learning difficulties or other special needs, and several organisations such as the Camphill communities had introduced refurbishing to their programmes, with well equipped workshops and an imaginative approach to education. For people who may otherwise feel marginalized, taking part in TFSR offers satisfying productive work and a sense of being part of a wider community.

Many groups also had the pleasure of meeting John Magembe from the Folk Development Colleges in Tanzania and Temba Ndiweni from ORAP, Zimbabwe. Each spent three months visiting TFSR

> *Working with young people day to day – I suppose one is aware that many of them come in in the morning preoccupied with their own unfinished business, whether it's about growing up or about troubles at home – just like lots of young people growing up – and the important thing is to help them reach out beyond all that stuff; and then the work becomes a background to the process which can begin to embrace whatever it is that they personally have to work out. It's put in a way that says, 'Look, you are actually having a chance here to do something very worthwhile, and your life is connected with the wider world – your life is relevant and you are valued as a person.'*
>
> *Working together here, restoring these old hand tools, feels like a form of alchemy. We see not only shining metal and honey-coloured wood emerging, but some transformation happens in the people doing the work. As we release the latent potential in the tools, there can come an awareness of where they have come from and the world they are going out into.*

PAUL TURNER, *GARVALD, EDINBURGH*

teams. Both were articulate and inspiring ambassadors for their countries and made a great impression on everyone they met.

Meanwhile, the character of the TFSR headquarters at Netley Marsh had also changed, with a separate machine shop and sandblaster, courtesy of local Rotarians, and a brand new exhibition area, complete with African forge built by Crickhowell TFSR. After five years as Partnership Worker, Ruth Heine married and left to start a family, and Jon Mussett took over the reins.

An interesting article in *Elbow Grease* compared the relative costs of tools in Tanzania and Britain. A locally-produced axe, for example, would take 11% of an African monthly income – and an imported one 38%; but a £19 felling axe would take only 2.7% of a fairly typical British monthly wage.

Expenditure for the year was greater than ever before (£239,527) largely due to increased tool production and overseas partnership costs (together: £89,500) and the year ended with a deficit of £7,484. But 52,589 tools had been sent out, which brought the cumulative total to 363,378. Meanwhile, the 25 village based units supported in Tanzania had hammered out 74,000 more tools and domestic items, thanks in part to the 36 tonnes of scrap lorry springs collected by TFSR volunteers. This brought the three-year total to 124,000. But the units were just getting into their stride. By the end of 1994, thirty units had turned out a further 160,000 items*.

1994 Mademoiselle in tears, a Roadshow and an All-Africa event

The highlights of 1994 were sending out TFSR's half-millionth tool and running the African Tool-making Conference, Competition & Exhibition in Ghana.

Neil Corney and Tony Care's visit to Ghana the previous year had introduced them to many local organisations. They were much impressed by the Jachie Training Centre (Kumasi) where students with disabilities learned guitar making, tailoring and orthopaedic skills. On finishing, they got good follow-up support, including tools from TFSR, to help turn their new skills into productive use. However, at a different vocational centre, a beautiful box of TFSR tools lay unused in a locked room while the Director asked Neil and Tony for more to equip some blacksmiths only 100 yards away. A little diplomacy, and they managed to liberate some of his hoard.

They visited many blacksmithing groups that often had poor equipment. One smith, lacking an anvil, was forging on a special stone from the river bed with skills passed down from his father and grandfather. However, Nana Abrefa, a smith in Kumasi, turned lorry half-shafts and axles into a wide range of excellent hammers. His high quality tools really could compete with, and beat, factory imports. (Within a few months Nana Abrefa was to win international prizes. See below.)

In February 1994, Belfast and Dublin announced great progress. The Belfast team, with Diarmuid Moore and John and Stephen Wood, had adopted the name 'Tools for Solidarity' and were moving their workshop from a friend's garage to a spacious building, formerly a flax mill. They chose the location carefully, so as to be equally accessible to both Protestant and Catholic communities, and the rooms were on the ground floor to ensure disabled

---

* Just how to define 'one tool' was sometimes a problem. If TFSR refurbishes a hammer, say, it's clear enough. But a brace plus a pack of ten bits: is that one tool or eleven, or what? TFSR would normally count it as two, since collecting, cleaning, sharpening and packing ten bits would take at least as much effort as would a brace. Likewise in Africa. A hoe blade is only part of the finished item, but if village blacksmiths spend a morning heating, cutting and shaping ten blades – they will count that as ten tools. And who can blame them? Also, the smiths might make lengths of chain, security bolts, cart axles and other items for field or home. Not exactly tools, but equally basic and useful, so they were included in the statistics. Finally, concerning the suspiciously round annual totals. These are probably under-estimates, based on the figures reported. The smiths were far better at producing tools than at record keeping. Often, there were gaps in their notebooks where weeks had gone by and they had not put pencil to paper, even when production had continued.

ABOVE Alice Matembo, Education Extension Worker, with one of the many women's sewing groups in Lindi Region, Tanzania (1985)

access. A grant from the Tudor Trust – one of TFSR's most generous supporters over the years – gave them a chance really to get going. The tools groups, north and south, had long been in friendly cooperation despite the Irish 'troubles'. As the Dublin team, with Tara Foley and friends, had no refurbishing workshop, they took all their collected tools to Belfast.

In May, TFSR noted that it had sent 4,103 reconditioned sewing machines to communities overseas since 1978. Some people, including Schumacher, consider these to be less machines than sewing *tools* since they are so basic and universal, but whatever the term, each is a small workshop in its own right. However, from feedback, it was clear that growing numbers of these machines were out of action, not because of any major fault, but because tailoring groups in Africa often lacked someone with skills to maintain them or make small repairs.

Thanks to a grant from the Clothworker's Foundation, TFSR was able to fund the first sewing machine refurbishing training course overseas, at the Kibaha Folk Development College, Tanzania. Eight trainees took part, all tutors in tailoring from others FDCs, under the guidance of John Magembe and Per Åkesson based in

Tanzania, and Markus Wahl from Netley Marsh – another in a long line of German long-term volunteers. Several more such courses were to follow.

Long-term volunteers (LTVs) played an important role at TFSR. Of course there were day helpers at Netley Marsh, and local groups all round the country who were purely voluntary. And most staff were semi-volunteer, in the sense that they worked for very modest rates of pay. These rates had improved over time, but one thing was certain: nobody worked at TFSR for the salary! However, the load at Netley Marsh was so great that TFSR needed, and welcomed, young people who would stay for up to a year, for board, lodgings and pocket money. Increasingly, they came from Europe, sometimes to learn English, sometimes as an alternative to military service.

The LTVs included Peter Effenburger, Florian Köhler and Marcus Wahl, but there were many more, young women and men from Germany, France, Spain, Slovenia, Trinidad, Ghana, Uganda and elsewhere, and their enthusiasm, energy and culture livened up the place. Often, they would focus on one aspect of TFSR's work – with Marcus, it was sewing machine repair – and as the year went on, they became skilled and able to visit TFSR local groups to help run weekend courses. Many LTVs left stories behind them. One French girl, for example, had come to England hoping to work with children in Birmingham, but the scheme had fallen through and she was diverted to Netley Marsh. She spent her first evening in floods of tears, dismayed by the stacks of rusty old tools. 'It is 'orrible,' she cried, 'I do not want to be 'ere!' But she stuck it out, and ten months later, returning home, she embraced everyone in turn. 'It has been wonderful,' she exclaimed, and left – in floods of tears.

On the staffing side in 1994, Judith Barrett joined as Regional Organiser for the Midlands and South East. Tim Blumfield – bearded crossword solver, pint sinker and Workshop Organiser – left for Australia, to be replaced by another Tim, Tim Young. With a background in engineering and fresh from a VSO placement in the Philippines, Tim was to hold this post for a considerable period.

June 1994 brought both great satisfaction and deep sorrow. In South Africa, the apartheid regime had collapsed and national elections swept the African National Congress to victory. Hopes were high, and for many people in TFSR – particularly the old-timers – it came as a vindication of their years of work against racism. On the day that Nelson Mandela became President, the new South African flag flew in celebration above Netley Marsh workshops.

But the flag had been sewn late one night by Glyn's wife, Sigyn, already

TOWARDS THE NEW MILLENNIUM 1991–1995

PREVIOUS PAGES The Half a Million Tools Roadshow hits Manchester (1994)

mortally ill with cancer and in great pain. It was her last gift to TFSR. Ever since her workcamp days in Europe and as a teacher in Nigeria, she had supported international causes, and in later years she had put her personal needs aside to allow Glyn to realise – as Michael Jacobs once put it – 'his obsession'. Sigyn died in June, still in her fifties and leaving three sons. Hundreds of friends and comrades gathered at her funeral and TFSR later planted a Swedish hornbeam for her in the Netley Marsh grounds.

Half a million tools – TFSR's travelling Roadshow

To celebrate the 124,000 tools made in Tanzania under the SIDO-TFSR programme and some 425,000 refurbished tools sent from the UK, directors agreed to hold a 'half-millionth' event in the autumn. For this, Mark wanted to do something rather special – not a single celebration but a travelling Roadshow. He asked the Ford Transit factory in Southampton if they would donate a shiny new vehicle. They replied, 'We get ten such requests every day; so probably not.' Surprised that Ford hadn't snapped up his offer to drive their white van the length and breadth of the country, he tried again. Think of the publicity they would get, and the moral uplift to be gained by helping a local charity! It was touch and go, but it did the trick, a Transit arriving just one week before the Roadshow was due to start. Judith Barrett packed it with display materials, clambered aboard and drove straight to Aberdeen and artist David Newbat.

It was impossible not to like David's optimistic colours and he produced something truly original for the Transit. Within hours he had sprayed, stippled and brushed one side of the vehicle, with a beautiful lightness of touch, and was finished. It glowed. Tools passed from a deep blue scrap heap to a brown workshop and then emerged into a golden African landscape. The other side, painted on a cold Sunday morning outside Manchester Town Hall, with David stopping off on his way to Germany, showed African smiths hammering in the dark by firelight, sparks flying from glowing metal, and finished tools being handed to villagers under green trees. Impressionist? Turneresque? Who can say! One thing is sure – as with the Netley Marsh mural, Harry Iles's sculptures, and the multi-coloured textile banners that groups sewed for events – TFSR brought out the creative best in everyone.

In this stunning new van, a succession of TFSR staff drove to celebrations and displays in Edinburgh, Carlisle, York, Bradford, Manchester, Bangor, Hereford, Exeter, Southampton, Norwich and

Leicester. At each stop, local TV and radio made effective use of Richard Briers' specially recorded TFSR tribute. Finally to Birmingham, where, in Victoria Square, on the 22nd October – in the only rain of the whole journey – a huge 'tools pyramid' and 6 metre-long (inflatable) anvil were set up. At midday, Bishop Trevor Huddleston presented the High Commissioner of Tanzania with our half-millionth tool, a mighty anvil. Then followed a *Global Any Questions* (including local MP Estelle Morris), a civic reception in the City Hall, and dance till the small hours, with world music by Caliche, Sekwese and the Afro Bloc Band.

With all the ups and downs of 1994, with a new floor added to the main workshop at Netley Marsh to stack hundreds of sewing machines, with 53,072 refurbished tools sent out (including 803 sewing machines) - one might have thought that TFSR staff and volunteers might be taking a little breather as the year drew to a close. But there was one more event to see to, the culmination of two years' planning, negotiating and fundraising.

At the 1992 Arusha Conference, Julius Nyerere had urged TFSR to extend the 'tools' concept much more widely in Africa. 'You can't address poverty without addressing the poor,' he said, '...people in the villages want tools. They'll need millions of hammers.' Glyn had agreed that working people know full well the need for tools, but stressed in his own talk to the conference that it was those in power – the politicians and administrators, North and South – who had the blind spot, and who preferred instead to spend billions on 'projects' and high energy technology.

So it was that four African partner organisations* and TFSR began to prepare the first-ever African Tool-Making Conference, Exhibition and Competition, to be held in Accra, Ghana, 1-5th December 1994.

> " *I belong to the York Hungry-for-Change group and we spend a lot of time discussing development issues, watching videos, going to Area Forums and so on. But you wonder after all that what you've actually done – and what appeals to me about this is the doing.*
>
> MARY MACHEN, YORK TFSR "

---

* Organisation of Rural Association for Progress (ORAP), Zimbabwe; Small Industries Development Organisation (SIDO), Tanzania; Association for Rural Development (ARD), Sierra Leone, and the Voluntary Workcamps Association of Ghana (VOLU).

ABOVE Bishop Trevor Huddleston, Mwalimu Julius K. Nyerere and Mr E.B. Toroka (Director General, SIDO) at the Arusha Conference (1992).

This gathering brought together tools specialists from a wide range of countries south of the Sahara*. Some were working blacksmiths; others ran tool-making support projects; others promoted artisans and crafts agencies, rural and women's groups, youth and voluntary service associations. All shared a common concern for the basic idea of African-made tools for African development. Harry, Mary and Glyn had the good fortune to represent TFSR at this remarkable event.

The conference itself took place at a beach complex, a few miles down the coast from Accra – not a Hilton, but a compound of traditional, palm-roofed huts (with no electricity the first night, and other challenges that generated both exasperation and laughter) and many

* Benin, Botswana, Burkina Faso, Cameroon, Chad, Congo, Gambia, Ghana, Ivory Coast, Kenya, Lesotho, Malawi, Mali, Nigeria, Senegal, Sierra Leone, South Africa, Swaziland, Tanzania, Togo, Uganda, Zambia and Zimbabwe

sessions were held out of doors under the palm trees, with the surf breaking only a few feet away.

Discussions highlighted the problems that limit African tool production still today:

- lack of interest by national leaders and aid agencies in supporting the artisan sector of the economy, especially local tool production

- lack of raw materials, especially scrap steel

- cheap imports of poor quality tools and other goods dumped in Africa under trade liberalisation pressures from the World Bank and International Monetary Fund

- lack of consumer confidence in African-made goods

- ineffective promotion and advertising of locally made tools

The conference came up with 39 practical recommendations for dealing with these problems, amongst them:

- more research into the types of tools wanted by local people

- improved tool production techniques – by a modest upgrading of technology

- blacksmiths to form Trade Associations

- improved promotion and advertising for locally made tools

- tool-making exhibitions and competitions to stimulate pride, improve techniques and promote sales

- invitations to national leaders and government officials to these exhibitions

- sourcing of steel scrap for smiths, and banning of exports of scrap to industrialised countries

- vocational training programmes should include tool-making courses

- Northern aid agencies working in Africa should purchase from African tool producers, rather than import industrially-made tools

The exhibition and competition were held at the British Council back in Accra and proved a lively and colourful affair. Each country had on display 20 of its best locally made tools. Some focused on traditional tools such as beautifully elegant digging hoes, razor-sharp machetes and tough agricultural implements. Others brought quality equipment for carpentry, metalwork, mechanics and building. Each country

LEFT Prize-winning hammers at the All-Africa Tool-Making Conference in Accra, Ghana. Nana Abrefa second from right (1994)

decorated its stall with cloths, flags, photos and the finest of its tools. An international panel of judges then had the tricky task of selecting prize winners, and eventually Gold and Silver Stars were placed on 35 of the very best exhibits, plus Certificates of Commendation – shared pretty evenly between most of the participating countries, though Benin, Zambia, Zimbabwe, Kenya, Tanzania and Ghana (Nana Abrefa's hammers, in particular) did especially well.

Overall, the message from Accra was crystal clear, and Mark, holding the fort at Netley Marsh, put out an immediate press release to the media. In essence, it was this: *Excellent tools can be made – are being made – in Africa, by Africans. If 500 can be produced for the Accra Conference, why not 500 million for the whole continent?*

It had been a wonderful experience, and participants went home full of plans for new activity. But it had not been easy. The Commercial Bank of Ghana traumatised Mary – carrying thousands of dollars to cover conference and travel costs – by claiming that her entire currency was invalid. (She fought back and prevailed.) The conference itself had nearly collapsed at one point, when long-winded speakers dragged it almost a day behind schedule. And Harry and Glyn both fell ill with food poisoning after a dodgy vegetarian meal on the plane back to Heathrow.

1994 had been a year of considerable ups and downs.

1995 *Wonderful Copenhagen and a new dawn for TFSR*

In early January, Glyn wrote to the TFSR directors, 'After sixteen years, full of interest, friendship and satisfaction, I now feel it would be better if I were to move on to some other work.' This was prompted by the death of Sigyn, a general sense of fatigue and the need, somehow, for a new start. TFSR itself was evolving, really getting into its stride, but Glyn knew of several other volunteer organisations where the person who launched and built them up had simply stayed around too long. They themselves relished the role of grand old man, but others found them a pain.

Directors accepted Glyn's resignation, as of 30th April, asked Mark to move across and take his place as Coordinator (Resources & Development) and advertised for a new Coordinator (Operations).

UN World Summit for Social Development

One of Mark's first tasks was to visit Copenhagen with Regional Organisers Judith Barrett and Neil Corney. There, they met up with Dutch and Danish tools organisations, to run a seminar and exhibition at a non-governmental Forum alongside the UN Summit – itself a follow-on from the 1992 UN Summit on Environment and Development in Rio de Janeiro. They enjoyed a prime site: thousands of people saw the tools pyramid and other displays and took the TFSR illustrated leaflet: *'Youth need work; work needs tools'*.

The Copenhagen Social Summit claimed that it wanted to promote:

- An enabling economic environment

- The enhancement of social integration, particularly of disadvantaged and marginalized groups

- The alleviation and reduction of poverty and the expansion of productive employment.

In response to these admirable goals, TFSR issued the following statement:

We challenge the World Summit to demonstrate how these aims can be achieved, so long as basic hand tools are not accessible to the majority of working people in the developing world.

Mark raised this question with the UK Minister for Overseas Development, Lynda Chalker, both in Copenhagen and back in London. Her response to most of his points was, 'Free trade is the *key* to development'. However, the World Bank and the International Monetary Fund, promoters of free trade, were destroying small producers in Africa and elsewhere – the very people they claimed that they wanted to help.

In the spring of 1995, TFSR joined Christian Aid's campaign against Third World Debt and the infamous Structural Adjustment Programmes imposed on the poorer countries, knowing that some supporters would consider this to be political. Others supported this stance – amongst them, three additional Patrons for TFSR. They were Susan George, who had researched and written extensively on the World Bank and Third World debt; Sithembiso Nyoni, founder and director of ORAP in Zimbabwe, and Archbishop Desmond Tutu of South Africa.

The TFSR Annual General Meeting in March was overshadowed by the sudden and tragic death of Peter McDermott, leaving his wife Margaret and five young children. TFSR was still a small organisation in terms of activists, and when someone died, it did indeed feel like a family loss to everyone.

At the AGM, Dorothy Cussens announced her retirement and was thanked for her years of commitment. Geoff Levy, from Andover and a regular volunteer at Netley Marsh for several years, became a new Board member, as did Harry Iles, who was elected Chairperson.

The spring issue of *Elbow Grease* reported that participants from the Accra Conference had now run their own tools competitions and exhibitions in Sierra Leone, Lesotho, Chad, Uganda, Gambia, Zambia, Benin and Tanzania. Impressively, SIDO (and, in particular, old colleague Enock Ndondole) ran 16 regional toolmaking competitions and followed this up with a national event in Arusha, with President Mwinyi presenting the prizes. This was encouraging news in what was to be the last Elbow Grease. It was followed by *Forging Links* – a better-printed magazine, with more substantial articles and an excellent 'readers post bag' section.

June 1st saw the arrival of a crucial new figure at Netley Marsh – Jan Kidd – selected from 100 applicants to take over the day-to-day running of Tools for Self Reliance. With a background of working in Malaysia, Kenya and Swaziland, Jan soon showed her considerable administrative and practical skills, reviewing TFSR's operational structure and staff workloads, and helping out at the summer workcamp.

The next weekend, 150 people turned up at Netley Marsh to say goodbye to Glyn. It was quite a gathering, with members of the very first TFSR collecting team, like Eddie Grimble, Charles and Sarah Hirom and Ruth Roberts meeting newcomers to whom the tools idea was a novelty. In a passionate speech, Harry Iles recalled all those involved from the early days, the hundreds of thousands of tools that had passed through the Netley Marsh workshop, and the workers in some of the poorest countries in the world who now used them. He summarised Glyn's role in this by saying, *'Through TFSR and your inspiration, so many of us have found a way to act, to keep our heads up, to understand where in the world we live and what we have to contribute, to struggle, to build bridges and to connect to the many people who are working for change. I would say to Glyn – if you wanted to change the world, I believe you have.'*

Glyn was grateful for Harry's words and the good wishes from so many friends, but was also happy to see the torch pass on into new hands. As Julius Nyerere had put it – 'To pass on the tongs is to sustain and perpetuate the blacksmithery'. The weekend included blacksmithing, drumming sessions, discussion groups, special kits to refurbish for Sierra Leone, a children's programme, and music for all tastes. It culminated with four funky saxophonists leading the crowd in a dancing procession around the darkened workshops, the brass and the steel echoing in the night.

Come Monday, a new era was to dawn for Tools for Self Reliance.

The Early Years in Hindsight

AT THE START OF THE STORY, Frank Judd warned Glyn Roberts that turning ideals into practical action would not be easy. 'You too will make compromises,' he prophesied – and of course he was right. But compromise is not always negative; it may at times be the better option. More to the point perhaps, is to enquire whether TFSR ever *compromised itself* by its decisions or policies.

Questioning Development argued that genuine development requires

- the empowerment of those at the bottom of the social pyramid.

- that ordinary people in the North and South share a common (political) interest in this empowerment.

- and that organisations working against poverty and powerlessness, especially volunteer organisations, should them-selves be frugal, egalitarian and democratic.

Tools for Self Reliance aimed to work for such development – how far did it live up to these principles during the formative years?

Empowerment

In terms of empowering those at the bottom of the social pyramid, TFSR surely did well – and continues to do so to the present day. It provided great quantities of tools: nearly half a million up to 1995 (in addition to those sent by sister agencies in Europe, Japan and Australia) plus hundreds of thousands more produced in East and West Africa. And by 'passing on the tongs' TFSR helped to sustain and to rebuild confidence within communities that might otherwise have collapsed. It also supported numerous training programmes in techniques, design, promotion and marketing, in various artisan trades.

TFSR worked with partners in some of the very poorest countries in the world, and chose to assist poor and disadvantaged groups – such as refugees, disabled people, HIV sufferers, women's self-help associations and disaster victims. Thousands of these set up small enterprises, generating incomes that helped to improve local living conditions. In some places businesses did indeed fail. At times the community was so poor that no market existed for a craftsman's products; and craftswomen could find cheap imports of second-hand clothing undermining their efforts at tailoring. But even there, most TFSR equipment remained at village level, and one can reasonably argue that a community possessing a kit of 50-100 good quality tools for making and mending things, even if it doesn't set up a profit-making concern, will be less vulnerable and more able to cope than a village with nothing but a few traditional hoes and axes.

It's a fair assumption that virtually every item sent by TFSR reached a manual worker at the bottom of the social pyramid. One of the beauties of 'boring old tools' is that they are pretty incorruptible. One village may steal from another, but it may also put the tools to better use. Some equipment may be sold between artisans, but the money stays in the village. Corrupt politicians and prosperous bureaucrats cannot readily turn simple hand tools into cash, and added value from TFSR did not end up in Swiss bank accounts!

Solidarity

However, the organisation was far less successful in its second aim: getting working people North and South to discover and express their common interest in empowering each other.

Despite an initiative from ORAP, serious socio-political dialogue scarcely occurred between TFSR volunteer helpers in Britain and artisans working for a living in Africa and Central America. TFSR invested years of work in development education – publications, in-house seminars, displays, public events – everything was geared towards raising the level of awareness among TFSR supporters in the hope that they would, in turn, seek a 'meeting of minds' with working people overseas. And some TFSR teams really tried, with introductory letters, sometimes in Kiswahili or Spanish, and group photos packed into tool kits.

Some refurbishers visited rural Nicaragua, Kenya, Ghana and Tanzania to make direct contact with village workers themselves. There, they certainly learned much at the human level, especially where they could overcome the language barrier. And they returned keen to renew their efforts and keep up the relationship. A few succeeded, but the task was enormous, as were language and cultural differences. Letters took months to exchange (this was long before mobile phones and the Internet) and often petered out at last. And village artisans overseas faced communication problems of their own, sometimes even lacking writing materials and postage stamps. A basic thank you note, saying that the tools would be put to good use, was pretty much the limit that most could manage, though a few sent more detailed messages.

Another obstacle to a deeper level of dialogue was surely the fact that people, both North and South, hesitated to analyse with relative strangers their economic and social situation, particularly in terms of power and politics, local, national and global. This exercise is not easy to conduct at the best of times, and to do so in a public or semi-public arena requires a huge measure of trust, which can take years to develop.

Some may conclude, therefore, that TFSR's talk of work in a spirit of solidarity was rhetoric, that the organisation lacked roots in the class struggle and its vision was ethical rather than political. Despite its cooperative and socialist leanings, TFSR gained only moderate support from left-wing associations in Britain, and a Marxist theorist might well have dismissed its approach as counter-revolutionary (or at least 'wishy-washy liberal') for setting out to improve social and economic conditions rather than use them to bring about the Revolution.

Nevertheless, with bodies such as the African National Congress, FACS in Nicaragua and ORAP in Zimbabwe – NGOs founded to empower their poorest citizens, economically and in terms of education and political awareness – the relationship was explicitly one of practical solidarity. In Tanzania, too, TFSR aimed to support cooperative and communal efforts, inspired by that country's policies, although not directly involved with the disappearing Ujamaa village programmes.

At a less overtly political level of contact and dialogue, TFSR made exciting headway, especially once members focused their efforts onto six priority countries and twenty partner

We appreciate your effort and pray for your work, especially when it gears to a wider struggle for a world with greater equality and justice.

BALIE MACKOTIE, *LUNSAR, SIERRA LEONE*

organisations. As finances improved, more and more activists from Africa and Nicaragua came to Britain, sometimes for a month or two, sometimes longer. During that time they travelled as guests of TFSR groups, and here the two-way communication could be fantastic. These visitors were usually well informed and articulate, with impressive skills both practical and artistic. A weekend shared with a UK local group left a deeper impression on it than a whole year's worth of leaflets, field reports and videos sent from Netley Marsh.

Also, when TFSR staff and directors made overseas visits, they often achieved a different quality of contact, as compared with 'official' Aid agency personnel. They avoided staying or dining at posh hotels, and settled for cheaper boarding houses or the YMCA. There were no air-conditioned SUVs waiting at the airport; staff travelled by bus or in anything that partner organisations could provide, with TFSR

> *This was one of the best conferences I have attended. Everyone was anxious to participate through to the end, discussions were frank and open. There didn't seem to be a superior or an inferior partner in the discussions. The Charter and the Action Plan were the product and responsibility of all participants as the conference went through the draft, point by point, and all the amendments were discussed and mutually accepted or rejected.*
>
> ALIMAMY P KOROMA, *CHRISTIAN COUNCIL OF CHURCHES, SIERRA LEONE*

sometimes paying fuel costs. This was not inverted snobbery. No one wanted to waste money on big hotels and neo-colonial trappings. TFSR visitors to Africa and Nicaragua probably still misjudged certain situations and trod on certain toes, but by and large it made for mutual respect and friendly relations. Invariably, partner organisations took the time and care to make such visits worthwhile.

This quality contact was especially valuable when it came to the conferences that TFSR organised jointly with its overseas partners. Trust that had built up through practical cooperation over the years led to speedier progress in discussion, and produced better ideas. By the end of a conference, conclusions really rang true, and all were ready to act upon them. The sense of achievement could be electric.

Finally, on the subject of sharing a common interest in empowerment, it is surely no accident that world figures such as Julius Nyerere, Trevor Huddleston and Desmond Tutu, who devoted their lives to empowering the poor, chose to become patrons to this movement of enthusiastic amateurs, with its underpaid staff working from a reconstructed dog kennels.

Organisational integrity

And so to the third and last principle, mentioned in *Questioning Development*, that the organisation itself should be frugal and democratic. How far did TFSR stick to this ideal?

On the frugality side, TFSR operated on very tight finances, often frugal to the point of meanness. For several years, Glyn was the only staff member paid anything like a normal wage while everyone else served basically as a volunteer. Costs were kept down in every way, scrounging building materials, using both sides of the paper when photocopying, using address labels to save on envelopes, travelling the cheapest way possible and staying with friends rather than at hotels. The thought of hiring a conference

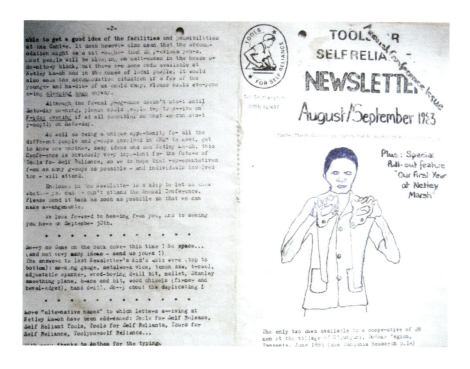

ABOVE **Frugality and self reliance gone too far? Note the stitched pages!**

centre for a gathering never occurred when a local school, church hall or marquee would do perfectly well. And frugality often, though not always, made for friendliness, pooled resources, improvisation and spontaneity.

It paid off too. After the initial bank loan, and three interest-free loans to complete the building work at Netley Marsh, TFSR was never again in debt, never in the red. Outgoings exceeded income in only three out of the first sixteen years. Then, TFSR drew from its reserves, firmly resisting any idea of going into debt to cover basic running costs.

But frugality could also be counterproductive. Some of TFSR's early, stencilled publications were truly awful, almost unreadable. Even strict Quaker donors, who rightly deplore waste, must have shuddered at getting them through the post. Better wages might have retained good staff members longer, and money invested sooner in the Netley Marsh site would have avoided much stress and brought in useful rents.

TFSR remained unashamedly lean and mean. It knew of NGOs that had accepted substantial extra funding, usually from government sources, with disastrous results: huge internal wrangles, money wasted (or worse), chaotic accounting, staff focusing on their careers and perks, and thrift laughed off as 'idealistic and unprofessional'.

On principle, TFSR chose not apply to certain sources for help with finance. The National Lottery was one, and so long as Glyn was fundraiser he always resisted seeking money from – what he considered to be – a giant swindle perpetrated on the poorest in society. The British Aid programme was another, during the late 1980s, when the Government cut its foreign aid and encouraged charities to help stop the gap.

However, it had not hesitated earlier in applying for government-level financing from UNESCO and the European Community. And by the 1990s, it did seek support from the British Aid programme to assist tool-making programmes in Africa. Double standards or pragmatism?

Now for democracy. Did TFSR make compromises?

The one big decision that possibly was compromising was to set up TFSR as a Company Limited by Guarantee rather than as a membership organisation. To have five director-members in complete control was in stark contradiction to the professed ideal of sharing power. It had great advantages, of course, in that a close group of dynamic people could achieve so much in a short time, but it skewed the organisation by fixing its direction and headquarters in the far south. Years of difficult debate would have been avoided if an open, nationwide, democratic structure had been chosen from the start. But who knows if TFSR would have done better to do so? Open to all, there might have been dramatic growth, drawing on the talents of many more people; but it might equally have become a talking shop, navel gazing and never getting any real work done. As it was, having laid the material foundations, directors did open up within three years, and members across the country were soon electing, and standing for, the board. As compromises go, it was perhaps not a bad one, and it has been maintained to the present day.

Some ideals were not realised, but that was not for want of trying. Once TFSR became democratic, supporters were not quick to sign up as members. For years, fewer than 60 did so, out of some 600-1,000 nationwide, and there were seldom more than 150 active members signed up, even though it cost a mere £1 to join. Of those who did, most would far rather clean up fifty rusty tools than come to an AGM, propose a motion, debate policy and vote. Nevertheless, AGMs were always lively, and attendance each year felt adequate (34 on average, 1985-1995, with a further 15 voting by proxy). Those who turned up usually had strong opinions. There were on average four motions put up for debate each year,

THIS ANNUAL GENERAL MEETING **notes with concern** *that a revised application form for TFSR membership has been drafted which excludes the preamble contained in the existing form, and* **proposes** *that any revised form of application for membership will retain the existing preamble, which reads as follows:*

"Tools for Self Reliance is a partnership of members and groups actively working for a more equitable distribution of resources and power in the world, developing personal links of support and understanding between working people in the industrial and developing countries. We also seek a better understanding of the need for and use of hand tools, and of the relationship of tools to society and the processes of development and underdevelopment in the world."

PROPOSED: **JAN HOOGENDYK** SECONDED: **DET GLYNN**, *APRIL 1986*

some raising fundamental issues. And that figure excludes the gruelling AGM of 1986, with 70 members represented – voting on 19 different motions!

Fortunately, at each AGM, three or four members offered themselves for election to the Board of Directors, committing themselves to hundreds of hours of meetings and paperwork – and this in addition to refurbishing work done with their local groups. They gave unpaid service, usually not even claiming travel expenses, at dozens of meetings and other events in the course of three years. Yet it is worth recording that virtually every one of them remarked how much they themselves had gained from the experience. More than one admitted – if that is the right word – that in some respects TFSR had actually changed their life.

As for African and Latin American members: at any one time they never numbered more than fifteen, falling far short of the 50% of total TFSR membership set as an ideal. This was disappointing, though in some ways understandable, given the problems of communication. And the precious few who did join brought wisdom and insight to the organisation out of all proportion to their numbers.

Some people have even felt that there wasn't *enough* compromise of democratic ideals at Netley Marsh, believing TFSR would have been more effective with a bit more hierarchy and

Over the years I have had the privilege of minuting the decisions of meetings of the Board of Directors (Trustees) of TFSR. In this time I have seen many changes of personnel and working styles and been impressed by their determination to steer the organisation through good times and less good times. In the early days we'd meet in the front room of one of the Director's houses, later in the house at Netley Marsh or an office somewhere on site. To make the organisation more accessible to its membership, meetings were organised around the country, with local members being encouraged to come and observe/participate in discussions (which few did).

In the early days the elected Directors tended to be active volunteers from groups. They not only decided policy but also had a say in the day-to-day running of the organisation. One agenda item that used to take hours (literally) was approving requests for tools. This involved a lot of preparation work by the Overseas Partnership Worker, but was valuable Development Education for the Board. The staff at NM produced significant amounts of paperwork to service the meetings, using paper of different colours for each topic. In an attempt to speed up decision-making, the Board set up 3 sub-committees, Finance, Employment and Development Education. This helped for some time, but getting volunteers for the first was tricky because few Board members possessed finance skills, and they several times co-opted financial advisers to assist them. Sadly this structure didn't always succeed in reducing the overall length of meetings, as Directors continued to debate recommendations from the sub-committees.

My job has become easier over the years, thanks to the advances in technology. Originally I'd take notes and type them up afterwards using correction fluid to cover my mistakes, as I had no spell- or grammar-checker. With word processing, things became easier and the final minutes looked a lot clearer, but still had to be done from my hand-written notes. Once, the Directors/ Trustees had to wait several days to receive a photocopy of the minutes by post. Currently I use a laptop. Minutes are ready almost as soon as the meeting finishes and can be e-mailed out the same weekend.

I often marvel at the time and effort put in by the Directors/Trustees as they work with the support of really dedicated staff, endeavouring to make the right decisions for the organisation. I feel it has been a real honour and privilege for me to be able to work with so many of them over the years.

TFSR *FROM THE PERSPECTIVE OF AN HON. SEC. EDDIE GRIMBLE* a little less egalitarianism. From the start, each member of staff took on some interesting tasks and some less enjoyable ones. Everyone typed/addressed/posted off their own letters; everyone joined the rotas for preparing the lunchtime meal, helped to stuff envelopes with the quarterly newsletter, cleaned the toilets, made tea for volunteers at 11am and 4pm, washed up and so on. The office staff would often leave their desks when manpower was needed on the workshop floor – loading a container, perhaps, and once spending a full day cementing parts of that same floor to get it done quickly and save paying a firm to do the job. But were these false economies?

The advantage of this approach was that everybody knew each other and appreciated the different skills needed within TFSR. It felt like being part of a team, and a happy and productive one at that. The Friday staff meeting, where each person reported on their week's progress and problems, reinforced this spirit. Days off sick were virtually nil – usually a indicator of good morale – and staff got through a colossal amount of work each week, quite apart from the many weekends when they would volunteer their time to run Open Days and similar events.

But some people (including a director or two) found the approach disjointed and unprofessional, and were not impressed to find the Workshop Organiser, say, spending hours upstairs pecking at a typewriter, or the Coordinator, not drafting mission statements, but downstairs on his knees unblocking the gents' urinal.

Some people may still argue that TFSR missed a great democratic opportunity in the mid 1980s, when it refused to allow Netley Marsh workshops to become a co-operatively run enterprise. A compromise of its principles? As mentioned earlier, two different levels of democratic control were involved, local and national. Each led to a separate conclusion.

And in early 1986, TFSR resolved its painful arguments for and against selling off Netley Marsh workshops, not by a process of Quakerly reconciliation, but by hard-headed voting, strictly according to the organisation's *Articles of Association* and *Standing Orders*, documents once thought laughably pedantic. In a crisis, they served TFSR well. Nevertheless, this 'imposed' democracy produced winners and losers, and didn't feel so good at the time (well, it *did*, actually – for the winners!), and the TFSR leadership soon set about rebuilding bridges with most of the disaffected.

One thing is sure: whatever the ups and downs, the pros and cons, *people really cared*, they spoke out and argued their case. At times, the debate could feel uncomfortable, even antagonistic, but it probably forged stronger ties.

OVERLEAF **All in favour of continued support to Sierra Leone! Annual Conference, Chester (1993)**

THE EARLY YEARS IN HINDSIGHT

Reflections on the past...

For us, TFSR was a significant part of our lives. Some of the things that made it so special:

- Working tools made a strong link between people, both tangible and symbolic.

- The size of the organisation. At times we considered adopting a nationwide 'Blue Peter' approach, but always decided that it wasn't for us. The quality of relationships was what mattered – the people, not 'Save the tools'. Over the years there has been little change in the size of TFSR, in the numbers of refurbishing groups, members, volunteers, staff and overseas partners. *Small is Beautiful*. The bigger the organisation, the more difficult it can be for individuals to feel valued. With TFSR, it was possible for us to know virtually everyone involved.

- The belief that development has to be on a human scale led us to a particular egalitarian way of working, with local partners, not expatriate staff, through good times and bad.

- The continuing inspiration of Julius Nyerere and his vision for Tanzania, TFSR's first priority country, and still a place of relative calm in a region which has known genocide and civil strife for 30 years.

- The challenge of combining the enthusiasm of volunteers and 'amateurs' with a sufficiently focused and professional approach.

- Enabling people of differing abilities to make a personal contribution, however small, to sustainable development and building a better world.

- The celebrations (personal and organisational), the creativity – artistic and musical – the conviviality.

- The pleasure of watching an idea spread, geographically to Europe and beyond, and also conceptually, to the point where 'seeds and tools', for example, are now an established part of many aid programmes.

The early years of TFSR show how any small voluntary organisation can evolve and manage change. It survived crises of staffing and funding, personality clashes, increased professionalism, centralisation and decentralisation. It kept going through arguments about democracy and the roles of staff and directors, lost tools, failed partnerships and disappointed hopes. Our story offers a picture of how a strong, simple idea, harnessing the energy and dynamic of volunteering, can produce and sustain a small, viable, development organisation.

For thousands, to work with TFSR was to experience a democratic spirit too seldom found in everyday life. How much production was made possible in small workshops abroad, thanks to efforts made in even smaller workshops in Britain? How many unexpected friendships formed over the years, and what new understanding arose of global issues?

… and the future?

This short book tells only half the story of TFSR. Since 1995, the organisation has seen growth and change, which we hope others will write about one day. In brief, TFSR is still going strong, training artisans overseas, developing projects with established partners, and sending out over 45,000 tools and sewing machines in 2007 alone.

But how relevant will it be over the next thirty years? The world we now live in is very different from that of the 1980s. Those were more hopeful times when most ex-colonies still seemed to be making progress and revolutionary movements in Cuba, Nicaragua, Zimbabwe and South Africa welcomed support from comrades in the North, support that we were proud to give.

Now we know that things are not quite so simple; even after winning self-rule, development on a human scale does not necessarily follow. Much of Africa has experienced appalling violence, under chaotic political regimes. Today, millions of refugees live in camps, surviving on food aid. Further millions of young people hang out in vast city slums, in hopeless unemployment. Under-funded public utilities collapse, or are bought out by private capital. Meanwhile, indifferent to the needs of their people, corrupt elites sell off their countries' minerals to foreign corporations and make more money from franchises on mobile phones, fake pharmaceuticals and alcohol. The silent Aids epidemic is still spreading.

Africa has also seen positive developments since 1978, especially in improved communications, greater regional co-operation, more children receiving primary education and the expansion of local NGOs bringing real benefits to their communities. And, of course, ordinary people make equally resourceful use of new and old technologies. Every few years, world leaders make fresh promises on aid, debt relief and new trade packages, though many are never honoured.

But now there is an even greater threat to Africa, indeed to us all, and that is climate change.

In the industrialised North our carbon footprints are huge. To reduce them, people swap their light bulbs and insulate their houses – but then go on as usual, buying and wasting mountains of imported food and clothing, driving everywhere, taking as their God-given right cheap flights, central heating and overstocked fridge-freezers.

Meanwhile, African farmers and artisans leave minimal carbon footprints. Few own 4x4s or plasma screen TVs. They eat food grown in local fields, they walk for miles, they make their own clothes, they waste very little – and they use hand tools. They do far more than their share to keep a healthy balance of CO^2 in the atmosphere. Yet they are the ones who will be worst hit by climate change.

But these same farmers and artisans, like millions elsewhere in the Third World, want to escape poverty, and have every right to do so. They dream of joining the consumer society, of driving cars, of enjoying 'The American Way of Life'. Yet *'The American Way of Life', squandering the world's resources as if there were no tomorrow, is itself a recipe for global disaster – ecological, social and climatic.*

What bearing does this have on development NGOs in the North?

If their focus is narrow (be it supporting women's credit schemes in Ghana, helping Aids victims in Zambia or planting trees in Namibia) their success will be short-lived when extremes of climate force whole populations to migrate. Even if NGOs broaden their perspective, urging richer nations to guarantee more aid, fairer trade and an end to Third World debt, they will still miss a critical opportunity.

To be 'part of the solution, not part of the problem', northern NGOs need to recognise that their own programmes also deepen carbon footprints, at home and overseas. And the more successful they are – for example, as improved seeds increase African village wealth, encouraging the import of cars, air-conditioning units and other consumer goods – the greater the output of greenhouse gases.

Is there some way that development NGOs can compensate for this? We think so. Alongside their mainstream activities, they can declare themselves unashamedly Green, in word and deed. First, they can audit their own activities to cut out waste and pollution, be it in materials or in energy – needless photocopying and downloading, the reflex purchase of another computer or office desk, questionable foreign trips. And, while putting their own house in order, they can make clear to the general public, to their own supporters and to Government that valuable development work overseas will be of precious little consequence if people in the UK and other rich nations do not move towards sustainable living – consuming less, polluting less. As Gandhi rightly said, 'The Earth can provide for each person's need, but not for each person's greed.'

RIGHT Carpenters in Nicaragua. Hard work, but non-polluting.

Criticising our own consumer society, urging more creative, less damaging ways of living, will not win many immediate friends. This radical message will need careful preparation, much as TFSR and others had to prepare their position on solidarity in the 1980s. Indeed, *this will be a message of solidarity* – with every southern community that is functioning sustainably.

To complicate matters, the British economy is now sliding into recession, if not depression. Some factors may be cyclical; others could well be linear. Global shortages of oil, essential for industry and transport, have already hit jobs and household incomes. The UK's lack of raw materials and its abysmal efforts to develop Green energy seem set to prolong the crisis, not for months but for years. Deepening unemployment and cultural poverty may spark off conflict between communities. A combination of siege mentality and donor fatigue would make it difficult for NGOs to rally support for, possibly, hundreds of millions in the Third World hit by drought, floods and starvation.

TFSR, though, might be better placed than most, with its clear focus on thrift, democratic relationships, low-energy technology, recycling and vocational skills. These could become key survival values in the 21st Century. By using tools to forge links of understanding and respect between communities, by emphasising the need for sustainable lifestyles, TFSR can help – in a modest way – to save the planet.

We have passed on the tongs, as each generation must. More strength to the arms of those who use them today! For our part, it was a privilege to share those exciting early years with so many good friends.

Appendix

Refurbished tools sent overseas by TFSR (1979-1995)

Year	Tools sent	Running total
1979	2,021	2,021
1980	4,708	6,729
1981	6,758	13,487
1982	2,502	15,989
1983	9,564	25,553
1984	15,345	40,898
1985	11,503	52,401
1986	28,660	81,061
1987	25,551	106,612
1988	24,905	131,517
1989	33,286	164,803
1990	49,826	214,629
1991	51,236	265,865
1992	53,346	319,211
1993	52,589	371,800
1994	53,072	424,872
1995	41,283	466,155

Tools produced under the European Community/SIDO/TFSR blacksmiths' programme, Tanzania, FDCs and others   284,000

LEFT Fine tools from TFSR Cymru

'You are instruments of hope for our rural poor, as these expensive tools are their only hope for better living conditions. [...] These are the tools for life.'

BEN SESAY
TARAMANEH FARMERS' ASSOCIATION,
SIERRA LEONE.

Keeping Something Alive...

BACK COVER PHOTOGRAPH **TFSR directors & staff (1990).**
Left to right: Tony Care, Kevin Petrie, Mark Smith,
Kate Sebag, Eddie Grimble (Hon. Sec.),
Robina Jordan (Chair), Judy Conner, Arthur Marsh,
Glyn Roberts, Mary Tolfree.